ICY
CREAMY
HEALTHY
SWEET

ICY
CREAMY
HEALTHY
SWEET

CHRISTINE CHITNIS

75 Recipes for Dairy-Free Ice Cream, Fruit-Forward Ice Pops, Frozen Yogurt, Granitas, Slushies, Shakes, and More

Roost Books
Boulder
2016

Roost Books
An imprint of Shambhala Publications, Inc.
4720 Walnut Street
Boulder, Colorado 80301
roostbooks.com

First Edition
Printed in China

♾This edition is printed on acid-free paper that meets
the American National Standards Institute Z39.48 Standard.
♻Shambhala Publications makes every effort
to print on recycled paper. For more information please visit
www.shambhala.com.

Distributed in the United States by Penguin Random House LLC
and in Canada by Random House of Canada Ltd

Designed by Toni Tajima

Library of Congress Cataloging-in-Publication Data

Chitnis, Christine.
Icy, creamy, healthy, sweet: 75 recipes for dairy-free ice cream,
fruit-forward ice pops, frozen yogurt, granitas, slushies, shakes,
and more/Christine Chitnis.—First edition.
pages   cm
Includes index.
ISBN 978-1-61180-289-4 (hardcover: alk. paper)
1. Ice cream, ices, etc. 2. Frozen desserts.
3. Milk-free diet—Recipes. I. Title.
TX795.C47 2016
641.86'2—dc23
2015009770

FOR VIJAY AND VIKRAM

May your lives always
be full of sweetness.

CONTENTS

A number of the recipes in this book are vegan, which means they contain no animal products. Vegan recipes are indicated by this icon: V .

INTRODUCTION

Nothing beats the heat like frozen treats. Whether you prefer ice pops or snow cones, frozen yogurt or slushies, there's no denying the satisfaction of digging into a frosty sweet treat on a hot summer's day. If you're a health-conscious epicure with a sweet tooth, it can be hard to justify that rich scoop of ice cream or sugar-filled pop, but there is a way to enjoy the best of both worlds, satisfying your sweet cravings while also keeping things light and healthy.

We're a family that loves desserts. Rarely a day goes by that I don't indulge my sweet tooth, and with two growing boys to feed, I am always coming up with healthy treats to help them end their day on a sweet note. What I've found is that there's simply no reason that desserts cannot be healthful and nutritious. Once you begin playing in the kitchen, experimenting with making sweets that are as healthy as they are delicious, there is no limit to where your creativity can take you. This can be especially true for frozen treats; focusing on in-season produce and high-quality ingredients will ensure that your ice pops and ice creams are delicious, light, and satisfying. For me this means sourcing dairy from a local farm, Fairtrade chocolate from reputable companies, in-season fruit from the farmers' market, and herbs snipped from my own garden. It also means relying on natural sweeteners such as maple syrup, honey, dates, and coconut sugar rather than refined sugar.

My family has become so accustomed to high-quality, homemade, whole foods–based desserts that my kids don't find much satisfaction in store-bought treats. Sure, they are sweet, but beyond that there isn't much in the way of freshness, depth of flavor, or texture. This only confirms what I have always believed: once you commit to whole-some cooking with an emphasis on quality ingredients, you'll never look back. This holds as true for desserts as it does for breakfast, lunch, and dinner. The beauty of making your own frozen treats is that you will be able to trust that every ingredient, from the dairy and chocolate to the fruits and herbs, are up to your own high standards.

About the Recipes

Here you'll find seventy-five original whole food recipes for frozen treats. Depending on your dietary needs, these recipes lend them-selves well to substitution. You can try substituting dairy milk for nut milk, or vice versa, and experiment with swapping in different sweeteners. Taste as you go; none of the recipes (besides those for the four cookies) contains eggs or other potentially harmful raw ingredi-ents. The recipes in this book are made for playing and experimenting, though if you follow them to the letter, you certainly won't be disap-pointed by the results.

A number of the recipes in this book are vegan, which means they contain no animal products. Vegan recipes are indicated by the icon v. There's a great debate over whether honey qualifies as vegan. For the sake of purity, nothing in this book containing honey is labeled as vegan. Recipes containing chocolate will be noted as vegan; check chocolate ingredients to make sure that there is no dairy listed.

BASIC TOOLS
AND TECHNIQUES

Here you'll find tips and tools that will guide you along as you make your way through the recipes in this book. Each of the categories—from ice pops to frozen yogurt—requires its own set of basic skills and equipment. That being said, the techniques are easy to master, and you can get by with very little equipment when making frozen desserts. You'll definitely need a blender, but you can make do without pop molds or an ice cream maker. In this section I'll point you toward a few pieces of kitchen equipment that will make the process quite a bit easier while at the same time arming you with techniques for getting by without a slew of kitchen gadgets. Additionally, you'll find helpful tips and tricks for making each category of frozen dessert. They may be simple tips, such as how to best loosen ice pops from their molds, but I promise they'll come in handy as you start cooking.

Making Better Bases

The most important step in making your own ice creams, frozen yogurts, and ice pops is achieving the proper base. The base is simply the unfrozen version of the recipe; it is what you will pour into your ice cream maker or ice pop mold. The majority of the recipe bases involve fruit and sweetener, along with a creamier ingredient such as coconut milk, nut milk, or yogurt. Smoothness is key, which is why a good-quality blender is important.

I use a Vitamix, which is arguably one of the best-quality blenders on the market. With a high-power motor and sharp blade, it produces creamy, smooth results without fail. It is an investment, but if you are someone who regularly whips up smoothies, ice pops, and nut milks, it is worth every penny. However, a standard blender or food processor will still work when making these recipes, though results might not be as smooth.

Beyond a blender, a high-quality juicer will produce smooth, pulp-free juice out of whatever fruits, vegetables, and herbs you put through the machine. The great thing about a juicer is that it minimizes the workload of juicing; just roughly chop your fruits and veggies and push them right on through. If you can eat the skin (apples, pears), don't worry about peeling; however, anything with rinds and tough skin (oranges, lemons, pineapple) needs peeling before juicing. I love experimenting with flavor combinations, adding in a nub of ginger for a kick, a handful of kale for nutrients, or a sprig of mint for depth of flavor.

If you don't have a juicer, you can make juice by putting the ingredients in your blender, whipping them up well, and straining out the solids using a fine-mesh sieve, though the results will be much less smooth than with a juicer. For a few of the recipes that call for more common juices, you can skip the step of making your own juice and select the best-quality unsweetened juice that you can afford. Some of the juices called for—beet and cucumber for example—are not readily available for purchase and will require you make them yourself.

Ice Pop Basics

Although making ice pops seems pretty straightforward—pour, freeze, and enjoy—there are a few tricks that will ensure your success.

There are so many ice pop molds on the market that it can be a bit overwhelming. The mold I used when testing the recipes in this book is the Norpro Ice Pop Maker, a very simple mold made from BPA-free plastic. The Norpro is designed to make ten ice pops, and there is a

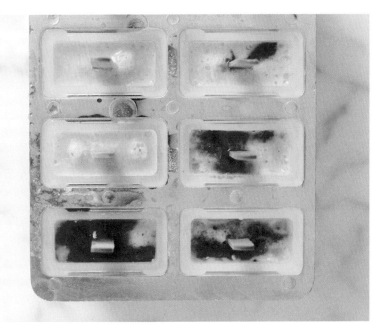

lid that fits over the top that securely keeps the sticks in place. While I try to limit the amount of plastic in my kitchen, plastic molds are easy to use, the pops are easy to loosen from the molds, and the whole thing is easy to clean; however, there are also several stainless steel options on the market now, and those could be worth investigating if you are trying to keep your kitchen plastic-free.

You can also forgo the pop mold altogether and use small paper cups or even shot glasses to make your pops. It's important to note here that different molds will create different yields; the amount each recipe makes is based on your pop mold. Note that when using glass, take care not to fill the molds to the top. You don't want the base to expand while it freezes and crack the glass or overflow into a sticky mess, so always make sure to leave "breathing room," at least one inch at the top of the glass.

Once your base is made, the next step is to properly fill your ice pop mold. Never fill your mold to the top; instead leave about one inch empty so that when you insert the stick, your molds won't overflow. If your molds have a cover, such as the Norpro, which holds the sticks in place, go ahead and insert your ice pop sticks. If your molds do not have a cover, then place your pops in the freezer for an hour, or until they begin to firm, and then insert your sticks. This will ensure that the sticks don't move around or sink in too deep. You want to push your sticks about three quarters of the way through the middle of the pop.

If you are hoping for a decorative flair with your ice pops, there are a few fun tricks you can try. When one or more colored bases are involved, layers and swirls are easy to make and result in beautiful pops. To achieve perfect stripes, pour a small amount of color 1 into the molds, and place them in the freezer for 30 minutes to set the stripe. Remove from the freezer and add color 2, return to the freezer, and allow to set for another 30 minutes. Continue alternating colors and freezing for 30 minutes to set each stripe. Be sure to insert your stick as you near the top. For a more abstract swirl, fill your mold about halfway with color 1 and gently pour color 2 on top, trying not to mix the two. Take a skewer and gently make a few figure eights through the mixture, swirling the two colors a bit as you go. Insert sticks and freeze.

Freeze time will vary for different molds, but it takes approximately 3 to 4 hours for most molds to freeze solid. Once pops are frozen solid, run hot water along the mold to loosen up the pops, twisting gently on the stick until they release. When using paper cups, simply peel off the paper starting at the top. If you do not want to eat the pops right away, you can leave them in their molds for up to a week. However, if you are planning to store them for longer, you will want to remove them from their molds and transfer them to a freezer-safe lidded container for fresher storage. Separate the pops with a layer of parchment paper so they don't freeze together.

Ice Cream, Sorbet, and Frozen Yogurt Basics

An ice cream maker is a fun kitchen tool to have on hand. In just twenty-five minutes, it produces the softest, creamiest homemade ice creams, sorbets, and frozen yogurts. I have a Cuisinart Pure Indulgence 2-quart ice cream maker, which is a simple, effective product. To use it, you'll need to pre-freeze the double-insulated freezer bowl. I keep mine in the freezer at all times so that when I feel like whipping up a batch of ice cream I don't have to wait. Once the freezer bowl is completely frozen, you place it into the maker, attach the paddle, and pour in your chilled base. When you turn on the machine, you'll notice the paddle remains still, scraping down the sides and redistributing the chilled portions of the mixture while the bowl rotates around. As the mixture is churned and chilled it thickens and ultimately turns into ice cream. The ice cream is rather soft, almost the consistency of soft serve, when it comes right out of the machine.

I prefer it that way, but for a harder ice cream, simply place it in a freezer-safe container and freeze for an additional two hours. Never freeze the ice cream in the ice cream maker's freezer bowl—you'll have to use an ice pick to get it out!

If you choose not to invest in an ice cream maker, you can still make ice cream, sorbet, and frozen yogurt. To do so, transfer the metal or plastic bowl that holds your base mixture into the freezer. After one hour, take out the bowl and beat the mixture using a handheld mixer until smooth, scraping down the sides of the bowl with a spatula as you go. The beating process prevents the formation of ice crystals, which ensures your ice cream will reach a creamy consistency. Return the bowl to the freezer and repeat the process a few more times until the mixture has reached an ice cream–like consistency. This will likely take 2 to 4 hours, depending on your freezer.

An important note: most commercial ice creams, sorbets, and frozen yogurts are soft and scoopable almost immediately when you take them out of the freezer. There are many reasons why this is the case, including the addition of stabilizers and additives and the fact that commercial ice cream machines churn more air into the ice cream than home ice cream machines. Since the recipes in this book are lower in fat than traditional recipes and don't include additives or commercial stabilizers, the ice cream will be hard when you pull it from the freezer. Allowing the ice cream to thaw for 10 to 20 minutes will return it to its creamy state, but I highly recommend serving the ice cream directly from the machine for the creamiest consistency. The addition of arrowroot powder in those recipes that don't include dairy products (see ingredient notes, page 17, for reasons) will help with the softness of the ice cream and sorbet, as will a tablespoon or two of alcohol if you choose. Both of these prevent ice crystals from forming and result in softer ice cream.

Flavored Ice Basics

The easiest way to make flavored ice is by purchasing a plastic sleeve specifically designed for this purpose. I use Zipzicles, which are BPA-free, and I appreciate that their zip tops close firmly and keep any liquid from spilling out. Unfortunately, they are not reusable, and as someone who strives for a waste-free kitchen, this does bother me, but I have yet to find a better alternative. I've heard mixed reviews of the reusable silicone molds, everything from leaking to an odd smell after being kept in the freezer for any length of time; because of these reviews, I have never tested these molds.

Once you prepare your base, which is essentially a thickened juice, you will need to transfer it into the flavored ice sleeves. For this I use a turkey baster or a funnel. Pouring directly from your blender or pitcher into the sleeve will result in at least half of your base splattered around your kitchen; trust me!

Snow Cone, Slushie, and Granita Basics

Snow cones, slushies, and granitas fall under the same culinary umbrella as flavored ices because of their icy consistency. Snow cones are made of shaved ice drizzled with flavored syrup. Arrowroot starch is used to thicken the fruit juice and a sweetener is added. This results in a thick, sweet syrup perfect for drizzling over shaved ice. Slushies are simply flavored frozen drinks—a broad definition to be sure—but that pretty much sums it up; slushies tend to be a bit icier than their smoothie and shake counterparts. Finally, granitas are made by combining sweetener, flavoring, and water and freezing until it reaches crystal form. For a perfect granita consistency that's not too icy, it's essential that you break up the crystals several times during the freezing process so that large crystals don't form.

When making a granita, you'll want to monitor it every 30 to 45 minutes, breaking up the ice crystals as they form so that the resulting dessert contains tiny, delicate ice crystals instead of becoming a frozen-solid sheet of ice. Pour your granita mixture into a chilled Pyrex or glass baking dish and place it in the freezer. After 30 to 45 minutes, ice crystals will begin to form around the edges. Use a fork to break up the ice crystals before returning the dish to the freezer. Repeat this every 30 to 45 minutes, using more muscle as the ice crystals become harder, for about 2 to 3 hours, until there is no liquid left and the granita has taken on its frozen consistency.

The key to great snow cones, slushies, and granitas is to keep the icy consistency light and fluffy. For the making of this book I invested in a shaved ice machine and discovered that it is quite a fun and useful tool to have on hand. Definitely not a necessity, but if you crave light, fluffy shaved ice that mimics the snow cones you get at country fairs and ball parks, you'll find a shaved ice machine will give you the best results. I bought the Electric Shaved Ice Machine made by Hawaiian Shaved Ice, one of the least expensive products on the market, and have been very pleased with the results. It comes with two plastic containers, which you fill with water and freeze. You then insert the block of ice into the machine and a sharp steel blade shaves the ice

as it rotates. You can also try a metal hand ice shaver, which requires little more than a block of ice and a whole lot of elbow grease! If you have a high-power blender such as a Vitamix, you can make "shaved" ice by simply throwing a handful of ice cubes into your blender and giving them a whirl on high power. The result will not be as smooth as shaved ice, but it can be a nice alternative if you don't choose to invest in a shaved ice maker.

When serving your shaved ice creations, you can simply use a small bowl or cup, though it's fun to serve them in paper cones. I actually prefer serving my shaved ice in a small glass Weck jar; you can see the syrup soaking into the ice, and it's an elegant and elevated way to serve this dessert. For serving, add about 2 heaping cups of shaved ice to a small cup or paper cone and drizzle the syrup over the ice just enough to color it but not enough to melt the ice, about 1/3 cup. Store the syrup in a glass bottle with a tight-fitting top. It will keep for two weeks in the refrigerator.

Waffle Cones

If you plan on making homemade waffle cones, you will need to invest in a waffle cone maker. You can't use a regular waffle maker for cone making, as the waffle grid is too deep, which gives you a waffle that is too thick to roll. A waffle cone maker has a shallow grid so that you get a thin, crisp, round waffle that you then can roll into a cone shape (most makers come with a cone mold). This piece of kitchen equipment is definitely a novelty, though if you love ice cream in cones, you'll have fun making and rolling your own. With your own waffle cone maker, you can make your cones to your dietary specifications, an added plus, as it can be very hard to find refined sugar–free or gluten-free waffle cones. Almond Waffle Cones (page 182) are both gluten-free and refined sugar–free.

INGREDIENTS AND BASIC RECIPES

The idea behind this book is simple: elevating frozen treats by incorporating farm-fresh ingredients—fruits, herbs, and even vegetables—into each recipe, while steering clear of refined sugar, dyes, and artificial flavors. The resulting frozen treats are unique, refreshing, healthy, and bursting with pure flavor. Many of the recipes are vegan, nut-free, and dairy-free, and all are free of refined sugar, instead relying on natural sweeteners.

Natural Sweetness

The recipes in this book rely on fruit and natural sweeteners including honey, maple syrup, dates, and coconut sugar to achieve their taste. For the sake of definitions, a natural sweetener is one that is grown in nature, harvested, and processed without the use of chemicals or enzymes. You will not find other popular sweeteners such as stevia used in this book because of issues I have with their taste and/or production. This is a matter of personal preference, and I would encourage you to play around with sweeteners to find your own healthful favorites.

If you are used to cooking with natural sweeteners, then you are most likely aware that they lend a different sort of sweetness to desserts than refined white sugar does. All of the desserts in this book are sweet but not overly sweet. You might find that when you are coming off a diet high in refined sugar, many of these recipes

will not be sweet enough for your taste. Relying on fruit and small amounts of natural sweeteners is something that will require your taste buds to adjust to. For example, if you are used to highly sweetened and flavored yogurt, a spoonful of plain whole milk yogurt will taste very sour and unpalatable. However, if you add a hefty drizzle of honey and lots of chopped fruit, you'll be able to enjoy the plain yogurt. The next time, you may find yourself using less honey. You might continue in this fashion until you find yourself enjoying plain yogurt and fruit with just the slightest dab of honey, or possibly none at all. You'll enjoy tasting the flavors of the fruit and the tang of the plain yogurt. In fact, when you then go back to tasting store-bought sweetened and flavored yogurt, you'll be surprised by the intensity of the sweetness compared to what you have grown accustomed to. This example extends to the recipes in this book. If you are coming off a sugar-filled diet, my recommendation is to taste as you cook and add more/different sweetener to bend the recipe to appeal to your taste buds, gradually reducing the amounts every time you try the recipe. Soon you'll find yourself enjoying the natural sweetness of fruit, with just the slightest hint of natural sweetener.

Here's what you need to know about the sweeteners you'll find used throughout this book:

COCONUT SUGAR A granulated sugar produced from the sap of cut flower buds of the coconut palm, coconut sugar has a rich, caramel-like flavor and contains naturally occurring trace minerals. It has a lower glycemic index than refined white and brown sugar and can replace traditional sugar in all cooking and baked goods thanks to its similar consistency.

DATES Dates grow on date palm trees, and while the fruit can be eaten fresh, they are mostly eaten dried. The Medjool variety are particularly prized for their large size, their sweetness, and their juicy flesh. The recipes in this book use dried dates, and although I recommend Medjools, any dried date will do. Soaking dates will make them much softer and easier to blend smooth. I soak my dates in hot water for 15 minutes, then give them a quick rinse and pat them dry.

FRESH FRUIT When you consume natural sugar in the form of whole fruit, you are also getting fiber, which reduces the negative metabolic effects of sugar. This is why sweetening with whole fruit, rather than fruit juice, is the healthier choice. For many of the creations in this book, fruit is at the core of the recipe. When a recipe relies heavily on fruit for its sweetness, it becomes critical to source farm-fresh, in-season fruit. Buying produce at the peak of ripeness ensures maximum flavor and sweetness; this applies to both fruit and vegetables. Once you begin focusing on cooking with in-season produce, the next logical step is to source it locally so that you can be assured of the quality, as well as the fact that it didn't travel long distances to reach your plate. Stop by your farmers' market or visit a local farm. Often farms offer pick-your-own options, which can be a great way to stock up on fruit while it is in season. Of course this doesn't mean you can enjoy these treats only during the spring and summer months when fruit is at its peak. Freezing fruit in-season, at the height of its ripeness, will ensure that you'll have the ingredients on hand to enjoy fruit-filled frozen treats no matter what time of year.

Tips for Freezing Fruit

- To prepare berries including raspberries, strawberries, blueberries, blackberries, cranberries, and currants for freezing, simply wash the berries, dry them thoroughly, and pick out any that have gone bad.

- For stone fruit including peaches, plums, cherries, and nectarines, wash the fruit and slice it, making sure to remove the pits as you go. If you prefer your smoothies and frozen treats to be free of the skin, you may skin the fruit prior to slicing.

- Bananas are a wonderful frozen item to have on hand for throwing in smoothies or churning up a batch of frozen yogurt–type desserts. To prepare bananas for freezing, simply remove the peels and cut them into thirds. If you have a powerful blender, you can freeze the bananas whole; weaker blenders may have trouble with whole frozen bananas.

- Many tropical fruits, including pineapple and mango, freeze well. Simply peel and core them before cutting into large chunks.

- Once the fruit is prepared for freezing, place it on a baking sheet covered with parchment paper in a single layer. Place the baking sheet in the freezer and allow the fruit to freeze thoroughly. Once frozen, transfer to a freezer-safe container. I prefer a glass container with a tight-fitting lid to ensure freshness.

HONEY A natural sweetener that contains antioxidants, vitamins, and minerals, honey is made by bees using nectar collected from flowers. Raw unpasteurized honey, which hasn't been heated at high temperatures, contains many more health benefits. Raw honey contains B vitamins, calcium, iron, zinc, potassium, and phosphorus and has antimicrobial and antibacterial properties. It can also help to soothe and reduce seasonal allergies. Finding a source for local, raw honey is easy, and it's worth the effort because commercially produced honey is often stripped of many of its health benefits during the pasteurization process.

MAPLE SYRUP Thanks to the presence of magnesium and zinc, maple syrup is a natural sweetener that contains some health benefits. Typically produced in Canada and New England, maple syrup is made by tapping maple trees, collecting the sap, and boiling it down into a sweet, amber-colored syrup. Choose from a golden color for a milder flavor and a dark color for a richer maple flavor.

Other Ingredients

The quality of ingredients that you use will directly affect the flavor and outcome of your frozen desserts. It is important to select high-quality ingredients that are in line with your culinary preferences. I like to shop organic whenever possible, and for chocolate, coffee, and other imported ingredients, I make sure to look for the Fairtrade label. As these ingredients become regulars in your pantry, you'll soon identify your favorite brands based on their flavor, quality, and integrity.

ARROWROOT STARCH Derived from a large perennial herb, arrowroot starch (aka arrowroot flour) is used as a thickener for soups and sauces. It has no flavor on its own, is naturally gluten-free, and stabilizes at lower temperatures (unlike cornstarch, which requires heating). It also stands up well to freezing. Arrowroot starch is used in two ways here: it is used as a thickening agent for the snow cone syrup, and, when added to ice cream or sorbet bases, prevents ice crystals from forming and leaves the ice cream softer and more scoopable. Arrowroot starch should be whisked and diluted with room temperature liquid. Recipes that use the starch will ask you to remove a tablespoon or two of liquid and whisk it with the arrowroot starch before incorporating it into the base. This will ensure smooth-ness. It is important to note that arrowroot starch does not react well with dairy—so any recipes that use dairy products will be free of arrowroot powder.

CHOCOLATE The chocolate aisle of the grocery store can be a sweet but overwhelming place. Dark, semisweet, bittersweet, milk choco-late, chips, chunks, powders, bars, nibs; it is safe to say that chocolate comes in all shapes and sizes. Chocolate is derived from the cacao bean, which is processed at a high heat, and sugar is added. There are a few important things to keep in mind when choosing your chocolate. This is a book that focuses on sweetening with natural sweeteners, but most chocolate contains refined white sugar. To make your own refined sugar–free chocolate sweetened only with maple syrup, see Maple-Sweetened Chocolate (recipe follows).

Throughout this book I use dark chocolate. There are no hard and fast definitions, but dark chocolate is typically defined as chocolate with no milk added and 70% to 99% cocoa. Dark is typically synon-ymous with semisweet, while extra-dark is bittersweet. The higher the percentage of cocoa, the less sweet the chocolate will be. If you feel called to use a sweeter chocolate in any of the recipes, you might try milk chocolate, though be aware it does contain more sugar than dark chocolate as well as dairy.

Finally, a note on Fairtrade: when you purchase chocolate prod-ucts that have been certified as Fairtrade, you are ensuring that the cocoa farmers have been paid a fair price for their product and that no slave or child labor was used during the process. Fairtrade also allows farmers to invest in techniques that bring out the flavors of their specific region. Fairtrade is a positive and sustainable label worth searching out.

Maple-Sweetened Chocolate
Makes one 6-ounce chocolate bar

*Many of the recipes throughout this book
call for chocolate chips or chopped chocolate chunks, but it can be difficult to find dark
chocolate that is free of refined sugar. Here
is a recipe for making your own chocolate
sweetened only with maple syrup. The result is
a rich bittersweet chocolate that can be used
for creating chocolate shavings and chocolate
chunks. It makes a wonderful replacement for
store-bought, refined sugar–sweetened chocolate chips and chocolate bars. Please note that
this chocolate does not work for recipes that
require chocolate to be melted, such as the Ice
Cream Truffles (page 193).*

> 6 ounces 100% cacao unsweetened
> chocolate, roughly chopped
>
> ½ cup maple syrup
>
> 1 teaspoon pure vanilla extract
>
> ¼ teaspoon salt

In a double boiler (or a metal bowl held over
a pan of simmering water), melt the chocolate,
stirring continuously to avoid burning the chocolate, about 5 minutes. When the chocolate is completely melted and smooth, add the maple syrup,
vanilla, and salt and stir until well combined.
Remove from the heat.

Line an 8 x 8-inch baking pan with parchment
paper and pour in the chocolate, smoothing it
out into a thin, even layer. Place the chocolate
in the refrigerator to cool and harden, about 2 to
3 hours. Once the chocolate has hardened, you
can keep it as a bar or chop it into rough chunks.
The chocolate will keep wrapped or covered in the
refrigerator for 1 month.

CACAO Cacao is the purest form of chocolate, produced from the cacao bean and minimally processed. Cacao is an excellent source of monounsaturated fats, cholesterol-free saturated fats, vitamins, minerals, fiber, natural carbohydrates, and protein that make it an excellent source of nutrients. It is one of the highest food sources of antioxidants and magnesium. You can purchase cacao in several forms including butter, powder, and nibs. Throughout the book you'll find cacao nibs and powder used with frequency. Cacao nibs are simple cacao beans that have been chopped into small pieces, and they retain all of the fiber, fat, and nutrients of the cacao bean. This makes it a healthy alternative to chocolate chips, which can be high in sugar and unhealthy fats. Cacao powder is made from cacao beans milled into powder at very low temperatures to protect the nutrients. This makes it a healthy alternative to cocoa powder.

COCOA POWDER Roasted cacao beans pulverized to powder produce unsweetened cocoa powder. Heat is used in the process, which diminishes the nutrients of the cacao bean. All of the recipes in this book call for unsweetened cocoa powder, which means there is no sugar added and the only ingredient should be cocoa. This allows you to control the sweetness and choose the type of sweetener you wish to use. There are two types of cocoa powder: natural and Dutch-processed. Natural cocoa powder is simply roasted cacao beans pulverized into a powder, which results in a light brown powder. Dutch-processed cocoa powder is cocoa powder that has been washed in an acid-neutralizing solution of potassium. The result is a dark brown powder with its acids stripped. This really makes a difference when it comes to baking—the acid reaction can affect the texture and leavening. For the purposes of this book, only natural cocoa powder is used.

COCONUT PRODUCTS The number of coconut products on the shelves these days is quite amazing. At most natural food stores, you will find shredded coconut, coconut flakes, coconut butter, coconut milk, coconut water, coconut sugar, as well as actual young green coconuts and brown mature coconuts. Here are a few things you need to know about the coconut products used here.

Coconut milk is used in all of the ice cream recipes as well as many of the other recipes. Coconut milk is the liquid that comes from the grated meat of a brown coconut, not to be confused with coconut water, which is the liquid found inside a coconut. Its pure white color and rich taste are attributed to its high fat content. You will find both light and full-fat coconut milk on the shelves. Most of the recipes here use full-fat coconut milk to achieve the proper creaminess, though a few of the lighter recipes call for light. I would not recommend subbing light when the recipe calls for full-fat coconut milk. The fat is needed to create the proper creaminess and richness. There are many coconut milk brands out there, but I prefer the taste and quality of Native Forest, which is organic and comes in BPA-free cans. You can also make your own milk by cracking a mature brown coconut, scraping out the meat, blending it with water, and straining out the solids, similar to the making of Almond Milk (page 29). Because mature brown coconuts are difficult to find and involve a lot of work to crack, I decided that I would stick with canned coconut milk, though you are welcome to experiment with making your own.

Additionally, you'll note that a few recipes in the book call for coconut cream. When you place a can of full-fat coconut milk in the refrigerator, the cream settles on top. A reminder of this is given in each recipe that calls for coconut cream. You can also purchase cans of coconut cream, which can be used in place of the cream that separates in the coconut milk. It is exactly the same, and no chilling is required with the canned coconut cream.

You'll also find shredded coconut used throughout the book—this is simply the meat of the coconut after it has been dried and finely shredded. Look for unsweetened shredded coconut, as the sweetened variety is very high in refined sugar and will alter the sweetness of your recipe. Toasting shredded coconut gives the ingredient a wonderful nutty flavor; toast coconut just as you would nuts (see page 24).

Coconut oil is used for roasting and grilling fruit as well as in baking. Look for coconut oil that is labeled unrefined as well as either cold-pressed or expeller-pressed; both extract the oil from the fresh, raw meat of a coconut without the use of chemicals.

Finally, coconut yogurt is a great product for people who don't eat dairy. The frozen yogurt and ice pop recipes that use dairy yogurt can be made with coconut yogurt, and the results are similar. Coconut yogurt is made from coconut milk, probiotics, and a thickener such as tapioca starch or agar. Straining coconut yogurt through a cheesecloth over the course of many hours will leave you with a yogurt that is similar in thickness to Greek yogurt. Experiment with different brands of coconut yogurt to find your favorite, and read the ingredients carefully, as many coconut yogurt brands are heavily sweetened. Or you can even try making your own.

DAIRY Finding a trusted dairy source is an important step for discerning cooks. If you are lucky enough to have a local dairy farm in your area, give them a call and make sure that their cows are free of hormones, antibiotics, and GMO feed. Animals should be free-range and allowed to graze. Even better if they use glass bottles, which are reusable and will not leach into the milk as plastic bottles can. If you are buying dairy from a grocer, look for labels that certify the product as organic, hormone-free, and rBGH-free. This also goes for yogurt as well as other dairy products you might enjoy, including buttermilk, cream, butter, and cheese. You can always experiment using nut milks and coconut yogurt in place of dairy products, though the results will vary slightly. The fat percentage of your dairy will also affect the outcome of the recipe, so I have noted the appropriate fat percentage in each recipe. Full-fat yogurt and milk will produce a creamier result, while skim milk will produce a more watery and therefore icy result. You can experiment with skim, 2%, and full-fat dairy products as you wish, but the results will vary slightly.

HERBS Growing a few pots of herbs on your patio or sunny window-sill can keep your kitchen well stocked throughout the year. I like to keep pots of rosemary, mint, and basil growing year round, as these are the herbs that I use most in my kitchen. I end up saving money, as small packets of herbs can be quite pricey at the grocery store, and I can be assured that they are grown without the use of pesticides. When purchasing herbs I find it much more economical to buy bunches at the farmers' market, where the portions always seem more generous than the small containers offered at the grocery store. Soft herbs (such as basil and mint) and sturdy herbs (such as thyme and rosemary) should be stored differently. For soft herbs, trim their stems and keep them in a glass of fresh filtered water, just as you would with cut flowers. Change the water every other day. I prefer to keep my soft herbs at room temperature, since I use them up quickly, and I like that they act like a bouquet and fragrance the air, especially basil and mint. However, if you plan to keep them for any length of time, you should refrigerate them in their glass. Sturdy herbs should be wrapped loosely in a clean, damp kitchen towel and stored in a lidded glass container kept in the crisper. Do not wash your herbs until you are ready to use them.

MATCHA Vibrant green in color and full of health benefits, matcha is a superfood made from finely milled green tea leaves. Matcha is the oldest variety of shade-grown green tea that has been deveined, destemmed, blanched, dried at low temperatures, then stone ground into a fine powder within oxygen-free chambers to prevent oxidation. It is then bagged or put into tins and flash frozen to preserve and protect its properties. Matcha should be kept chilled. Because you are ingesting the whole green tea leaf rather than just the brewed water, you consume ten to fifteen times the nutrients found in brewed green teas. Matcha is packed with antioxidants and fiber and acts as a powerful detoxifier.

Toasted Nuts
Makes 2 cups

As a fair amount of recipes in this book call for nuts, achieving the perfect toasted nut is an important step in the cooking process. While some might prefer to toast their nuts on the stovetop in a cast-iron skillet, I've found that using a baking sheet in the oven gives the nuts a uniform and even toastiness. While the time given is simply a guideline, please note that all ovens have slightly different cooking speeds despite set temperatures, and nuts can quickly go from toasty to burnt. Your senses are the best indicator of when the nuts are done; they should have a fragrant smell and a toasty look. While coconut is not a member of the nut family, the same rules for toasting apply. You can toast shredded or flaked coconut using this recipe, but decrease the baking time to 6 to 8 minutes. Remove the coconut as soon as it begins to brown, as coconut can quickly burn.

2 cups raw whole nuts or shredded or flaked unsweetened coconut

Preheat the oven to 300°F. Spread the nuts evenly on a baking sheet in a single layer. Bake for 15 minutes, giving the pan a quick shake or two at the halfway point. The nuts are done when they have achieved a toasty brown color and fragrant smell. Be extra watchful during the last few minutes of cooking, as nuts can quickly begin to burn.

NUTS Nuts are used heavily throughout the book in a variety of ways: Cashew Cream (page 27) is used as a base for the dairy-free ice creams, almond milk and almond butter (pages 29 and 30) add a creamy richness to many recipes, and toasted nuts are used as a topping or mix-in to give a nice crunch to an otherwise creamy dessert.

It is important to purchase high-quality nuts from a trusted source. I buy nuts in bulk from my local food co-op, where I can be assured that they are organic, and I always buy fresh nuts, never roasted or salted. I prefer to do my own toasting and flavoring at home, and it is important to use raw nuts for nut milks. As soon as I get home from the store, I transfer my nuts to a lidded glass container and store them in the refrigerator; this keeps them fresh longer and prevents them from going rancid.

SALT There are several types of salt, though I'll simply highlight two common categories without getting into specialty and flavored salts: table salt, which comes from salt mines, and sea salt, which comes from evaporated seawater. For the purpose of this book, I mainly use fine-grain sea salt, as I prefer the taste, though for a few recipes, such as the Banana Bites (page 62), I use large flake sea salt. Flake salt is typically thought of as a "finishing salt," which means it dissolves quickly and provides a nice crunch and a short burst of flavor. Delicate flakes are perfect for desserts in which you want to taste the saltiness but in a mild and sophisticated way. Flake salt is made from seawater, evaporated by the sun and wind, and then heated until crystals form.

SPICES You might not think of spices as kitchen items with expiry dates, but it is important to keep your spices fresh in order to assure their flavor and strength. Once a year—perhaps set a date at the beginning of each New Year—sort through your spice shelf and compost any spices that are past their expiry date or that have been sitting on your shelf for more than a year. If you are making a recipe that calls for just a teaspoon or two of a spice that you do not commonly use, you might try the bulk bins of your local natural foods store, where you can buy scant amounts instead of investing in an expensive bottle. I prefer buying organic spices because I can be assured that no pesticides or herbicides were used during their growth and that no irradiation or fumigation was used during their processing.

VANILLA Two vanilla products are used throughout the book: whole vanilla beans and pure vanilla extract. Vanilla beans are long, thin, brown beans that when slit lengthwise reveal tiny black seeds, which you can scrape from the bean using the tip of a knife. The vanilla seeds impart a strong vanilla flavor. Vanilla beans are costly, and many of my recipes call for this ingredient; you can cut the beans in half without compromising much flavor to help your beans stretch further. Store beans in a tightly lidded glass spice jar to keep them from drying out. Pure vanilla bean extract is made by allowing whole vanilla beans to macerate and percolate in a solution of ethyl alcohol and water. The label "pure" is monitored by the FDA and assures the ratio of alcohol to vanilla bean.

Basic Recipes

Here you will find recipes for basic ingredients that are used throughout the book: cashew cream, almond milk, and almond butter. It's perfectly fine to use store-bought almond milk and butter if you're not interested in making your own; cashew cream, however, can't be purchased premade. Homemade nut and seed milks and butters have the added bonus of being completely free of preservatives and additives, and you can control the quality of the ingredients as well as the sweetness and flavor. Use these recipes as a jumping-off point. Experiment with other seeds and nuts such as hazelnuts, hemp seeds, and macadamia nuts, as well as add-ins and flavorings such as pure vanilla extract, honey, maple syrup, dates, and cacao powder for sweetened and flavored milks and butters.

CASHEW CREAM

Makes 1 cup

This is one type of nut milk that you won't find on grocery store shelves. Luckily, making your own is quite simple. Soaking the cashews renders them soft and pliable and easy to blend. You can adjust the amount of water depending on how creamy you'd like your milk. This recipe will give you a thick, creamy product that is the right consistency to use in the dairy-free ice cream base.

1 cup cold filtered water, plus more for soaking
1 cup whole cashews
¼ teaspoon salt

1 Place the cashews in a bowl and add enough cold filtered water to cover them completely. Cover the bowl and place in the refrigerator overnight to soak.

2 Drain the cashews and rinse them well. Place them in a blender with 1 cup cold filtered water and the salt and blend on high speed for several minutes, until very smooth.

3 If you're not using a high-speed blender (which creates an ultra-smooth cream), strain the cashew cream through a fine-mesh sieve or cheesecloth. You want a creamy consistency with no solids remaining.

4 Stored in a lidded glass jar, the cream will keep for up to 1 week in the refrigerator.

ALMOND MILK

Makes 4 cups

It used to be quite difficult to buy almond milk that was free of additives and preservatives, and though you can now find a few new brands with ingredients that are nothing more than almonds and purified water, I still prefer making my own. It is both simple and economical. You'll find almond milk used in many recipes throughout the book, so make a double portion and store it in a large mason jar while you work your way through the recipes.

4 cups cold filtered water, plus more for soaking
1 cup raw almonds
¼ teaspoon salt

1 Place the almonds in a bowl and add enough cold filtered water to cover them completely. Cover the bowl and place it in the refrigerator overnight to soak.

2 Drain the almonds and rinse them well. Place them in a blender with 4 cups cold filtered water and the salt and blend on high speed for several minutes, until very smooth. Strain the mixture through cheesecloth into a wide-mouth glass jar (mason jars work well), squeezing the cheesecloth to extract all of the liquid. Compost the solids.

3 Stored in a lidded glass jar, the milk will keep for up to 1 week in the refrigerator.

ALMOND BUTTER

Makes 1 1/2 cups

With a bit of patience and ten minutes set aside, you can easily turn a handful of almonds into a creamy, delicious nut butter. Buying raw almonds in bulk and keeping them in a sealed glass jar in your refrigerator is a great way to ensure that you always have the ingredients on hand to whip up a quick batch of nut butter. Have fun experimenting with this recipe—add a tablespoon of honey and vanilla or a dash of maple syrup and cinnamon for a sweeter almond butter.

3 cups toasted unsalted almonds (page 24)
1 teaspoon salt

1 Place the almonds and salt in a food processor fitted with an "S" blade and process on high speed until the almonds begin to form a ball, 1 to 2 minutes. Scrape the sides down with a spatula, and continue processing until the mixture becomes creamy. This can take anywhere from 8 to 12 minutes depending on the power of your food processor and the sharpness of the blade. Be aware that older food processors may overheat during the process, so proceed carefully; every minute or so, stop the machine and use a spatula to scrape down the sides. Scoop the almond butter into a lidded glass container (mason jars work well) and store for up to 2 weeks in the refrigerator.

ICE POPS

ICE POPS SHOULD BE CONSIDERED one of the five food groups come summertime. They're perfect for backyard barbecues and hot days spent by the pool, and there are endless flavor combinations just waiting to be explored. Basically, if you can blend it up and pour it, you can make it into a pop!

In this section you'll find flavor pairings that are old favorites, such as peaches and cream and strawberry and basil, as well as a few surprise combinations including cucumber, melon, and mint. Once you've whipped and blended your way through these recipes, I hope you'll be inspired to experiment with flavor pairings of your own.

STRAWBERRY AND SWEET BASIL CREAM POPS

Makes 12 pops

Strawberries are the sweet and juicy reward for making it through another New England winter. When the first bushels of strawberries appear at the farmers' market, it's a sure sign that spring is in the air. Here, strawberries join forces with freshly picked basil for a decidedly spring-themed pop.

1½ cups full-fat coconut milk (from one 13.5-ounce can)

1 frozen banana

4 tablespoons honey, divided

1½ cups hulled and chopped strawberries

4 basil leaves

1 tablespoon water

1 vanilla bean

1 In a blender, combine the coconut milk, banana, and 3 tablespoons of the honey and blend until completely smooth. Pour into a pitcher and set aside.

2 In a small saucepan, combine the strawberries, basil, water, and the remaining 1 tablespoon honey. Slice open the vanilla bean lengthwise, scrape the seeds into the saucepan, and then add the bean itself. Place over medium heat, bring to a simmer, and cook, stirring frequently, until the mixture becomes fragrant and the berries begin to soften and give off their juices, 5 to 8 minutes.

3 Take the pan off the heat and remove and compost the vanilla bean and basil leaves (if you prefer a strong basil flavor, you may leave them in). Transfer the mixture to the blender and blend until just mixed.

4 Pour a small amount of the strawberry mixture into each pop mold and top with the coconut mixture. Insert sticks and place in the freezer for at least 3 to 4 hours, until hardened.

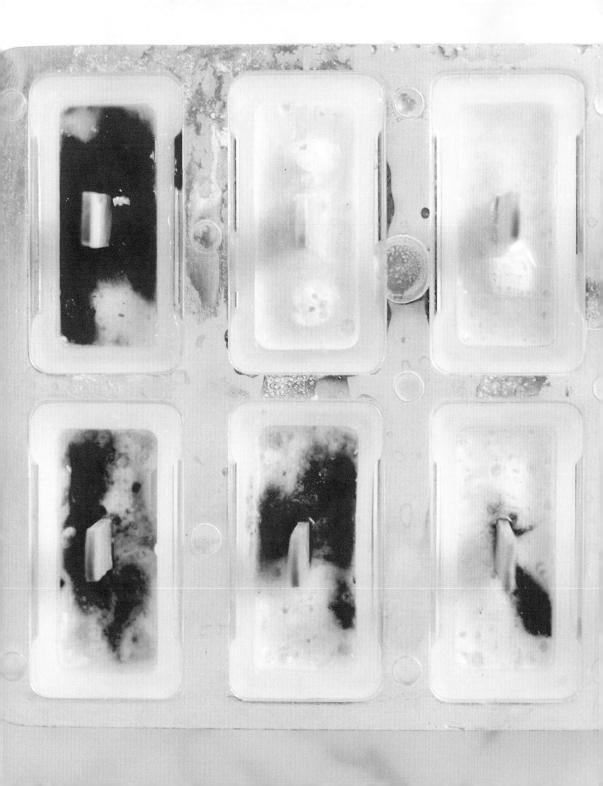

FIRECRACKER POPS

Makes 12 pops

These pops, with their bright stripes of red and blue, bring to mind the Fourth of July. I'm always amazed by the vibrancy nature provides, eliminating the need for food coloring or dyes. Raspberries create the bright red stripes, while blueberries impart their gorgeous bluish-purple hue for the alternating stripes. Bananas and a dash of honey sweeten the deal, while plain whole milk yogurt provides the creaminess. Feel free to use Greek yogurt if you prefer a bit more of a tang. These festive, colorful, and delicious pops are always a crowd pleaser.

1 cup frozen blueberries

2 frozen bananas

1 cup plain whole milk yogurt, divided

½ cup almond milk, homemade (page 29) or store-bought

1 tablespoon honey, divided

1 cup frozen raspberries

1 In a blender, combine the frozen blueberries, 1 banana, ½ cup of the yogurt, ¼ cup of the almond milk, and ½ tablespoon of the honey and blend until smooth. Pour into a pitcher or glass measuring cup and give your blender a quick rinse.

2 Combine the frozen raspberries and the remaining banana, ½ cup yogurt, ¼ cup almond milk, and ½ tablespoon honey in the rinsed-out blender and blend until smooth.

3 Pour a small amount of the raspberry mixture into your pop molds, followed by a small amount of the blueberry mixture and alternate until the molds are full. For the most part the stripes will hold their place, as the mixture will be thick (work quickly before they have a chance to thaw and become runny); however, if you want perfect stripes, you can stick the molds in the freezer for 30 minutes after every stripe to set the color before adding the next stripe. Insert sticks and freeze for at least 3 to 4 hours, until hardened.

ROASTED PEACHES
AND CREAM POPS

Makes 12 pops

Nothing compares to a farm-fresh peach, the kind that sends juice cascading down your chin. For this pop, it is important to choose the juiciest, ripest, sweetest peaches you can find. Steer clear of peaches that are hard or mealy. Roasting peaches with a bit of coconut oil and honey amplifies their natural sweetness. And when layered with slightly sweetened yogurt, the result is a deliciously creamy pop.

3 tablespoons honey, divided
1 tablespoon coconut oil
¼ cup water
4 peaches, halved and pitted
1 cup plain whole milk yogurt
1 teaspoon pure vanilla extract

1 Preheat the oven to 400°F.

2 In a shallow baking dish, combine 1 tablespoon of the honey with the coconut oil and water. Place the peaches flesh side up in the baking dish and roast until they are tender, 12 to 14 minutes.

3 Allow the peaches to cool in their juices until they are cool enough to handle, then slip the skins off (they should come off easily after roasting) and roughly chop the flesh. Fill each pop mold loosely with the chopped peaches and a bit of the juice from the roasting pan.

4 In a small bowl, combine the yogurt, the remaining 2 tablespoons honey, and the vanilla and stir until well mixed. Pour the yogurt cream over the peaches, filling each pop mold. Use a skewer to swirl the cream so it mixes slightly with the peaches, but do not mix completely. Insert sticks and place the molds in the freezer for at least 3 to 4 hours, until hardened.

BLACK FOREST POPS WITH HOMEMADE CHERRY COMPOTE

Makes 10 pops

The essence of Black Forest, when you pare it down to the flavors at work, is the luscious combination of rich chocolate, vanilla cream, and dark sweet cherries. The beauty of those flavors can get lost in the layers of whipped cream and overly sweet, brightly dyed maraschino cherries that seem to be synonymous with many store-bought Black Forest cakes. But staying true to the flavors and using high-quality ingredients, most notably dark sweet cherries simmered down into a rich compote, creates a decadent and creamy pop.

One 13.5-ounce can full-fat coconut milk

1/3 cup unsweetened cocoa powder

1/2 cup plus 2 tablespoons honey, divided

1 teaspoon pure vanilla extract

2 cups pitted and chopped sweet dark cherries

1 tablespoon water

1 For the chocolate layer: In a small saucepan, combine half of the coconut milk with the cocoa powder and 1/4 cup of the honey. Place over medium heat, bring to a simmer, and cook, stirring constantly to avoid burning, until thoroughly blended. Remove from the heat and let cool.

2 For the vanilla layer: In a small saucepan, combine the remaining coconut milk with the vanilla and 1/4 cup of the remaining honey. Place over medium heat, bring to a simmer, and cook, stirring constantly to avoid burning, until thoroughly blended. Remove from the heat and let cool.

3 For the cherry compote: In a small saucepan, combine the cherries, water, and the remaining 2 tablespoons honey. Place over medium heat, bring to a simmer, and cook, stirring gently, for 3 to 5 minutes, until the cherries soften and begin to release their juices. Remove from the heat and allow the mixture to cool and thicken.

4 Begin filling your pop molds first with the cherry compote layer, followed by the vanilla layer, then the chocolate layer. After filling the pop molds, take a skewer and gently swirl the layers together, being careful not to completely mix them. If you prefer stripes (like the ones pictured), freeze each layer for 30 minutes before adding the next layer. Insert sticks and freeze for 3 to 4 hours, until hardened.

BLACKBERRY COCONUT CHIA POPS

Makes 8 pops

Chia seeds are known as a superfood, meaning these tiny black dots are packed with health benefits thanks to the presence of omega-3 fatty acids, antioxidants, and fiber. When mixed with liquid and allowed to sit, the outer layer of the seeds swells to form a gel. In many vegan recipes, you'll find chia seeds used as an egg substitute, but in this pop, we're going for a pudding-like consistency, achieved by mixing the seeds with sweetened coconut milk and allowing them to sit until they swell.

4 tablespoons honey, divided

One 13.5-ounce can light coconut milk

3 tablespoons chia seeds

2 cups blackberries

1 In a small bowl, whisk 2 tablespoons of the honey into the coconut milk and stir in the chia seeds. Allow to sit for 20 minutes.

2 While the chia mixture is resting, combine the remaining 2 tablespoons honey and the blackberries in a small saucepan. Place over medium heat, bring to a light simmer, and cook for 3 to 5 minutes, allowing the berries to break down and their juices to begin flowing and mixing well to incorporate the honey. Remove from the heat and mash the berries. Allow the mixture to cool slightly, then push it through a fine-mesh sieve into a bowl to remove the seeds.

3 Begin making pops by adding a layer of the chia mixture followed by a layer of the blackberry mixture. For perfect stripes, allow each layer to harden for about 30 minutes in the freezer before gently adding the next layer. Insert sticks and freeze for at least 3 to 4 hours, until hardened.

WHOLE FRUIT POPS v

Makes 10 pops

Whole fruit suspended in coconut water creates a beautiful and sophisticated pop. These are almost too pretty to eat, and yet the simple, hydrating base of coconut water is too refreshing to resist on a steamy summer's day. The fruit chunks become quite hard when frozen, but as you work your way through the pop, they begin to thaw, becoming easier to eat. If you are serving these to small children, I recommend cutting the fruit into very small chunks, which will give the pop more of a "fruit salad" look and make for a safer experience for little ones.

1 kiwi
1 peach
¼ cup blueberries
¼ cup raspberries
3 cups coconut water

1 Begin by prepping the fruit: peel the kiwi and slice it into thin rounds. Cut the peach into small half-moon slices. Wash the berries well.

2 Pour enough coconut water in each pop mold to fill it halfway. Drop a peach slice, a blueberry, a raspberry, and a kiwi round into each pop mold. If needed, add a bit more coconut water to fill the molds. Insert sticks carefully, as not to smash the fruit, and freeze for at least 3 to 4 hours, until hardened.

GREEN MONSTER POPS v

Makes 10 pops

When it comes to getting my daily greens, I'll try just about anything. While I love big, crunchy, straight-from-the-garden salads, I also love blending my greens into smoothies. Sweet, creamy, and refreshing, it only makes sense that a blended green smoothie would work perfectly in pop form. Feel free to experiment with the greens: I prefer spinach because the taste is very subtle, but Swiss chard and kale also work well, though their flavors are a bit more distinct. I love the sweetness of freshly made pineapple juice, though you can feel free to substitute ready-made juice. If you're serving these to kids, play up the cool green color, and before long, they'll be slurping up their daily serving of health-infusing greens!

½ pineapple, peeled, cored, and chopped (or substitute 1 cup pineapple juice)

2 bananas

1 cup peeled, cored, and chopped mango

1 cup full-fat coconut milk (from one 13.5-ounce can)

1½ cups baby spinach

1 Put the roughly chopped pineapple chunks through a juicer. Measure 1 cup of pineapple juice (or use store-bought pineapple juice) and add it to a blender with the bananas, mango, coconut milk, and baby spinach. Blend until smooth.

2 Carefully pour the smoothie mix into pop molds, insert sticks, and freeze for at least 3 to 4 hours, until hardened.

CUCUMBER MELON MINT POPS v

Makes 10 pops

The alternative name for these lovely green pops would have to be Spa Pops. I can imagine being handed one after coming from a relaxing, rejuvenating massage. The pop has an understated sweetness with just a hint of mint. By juicing the produce rather than blending it, the consistency of the pop is very smooth, with no pulp to distract from the simple medley of flavors. This is one recipe where using a juicer is highly recommended, as blending and straining the ingredients will not result in the desired smoothness and consistency. Cucumber has incredible hydrating properties, as does honeydew, while mint is cooling and great for soothing the stomach.

2 cucumbers, peeled and cut into chunks

1 cup peeled, seeded, and chopped honeydew

¼ cup packed mint leaves

1 Press the cucumbers, honeydew, and mint through a juicer and stir the juices until combined. Pour the liquid into pop molds, insert sticks, and freeze for at least 3 to 4 hours, until hardened.

ORANGE COCONUT CREAMSICLES

Makes 10 pops

Do you remember when the ice cream truck would come tinkling down the block? There was no sweeter sound on a hot summer's evening. I was always stuck with the dilemma of what to order, chocolaty pop or fruity pop? These were the big questions of my youth. If I decided on the fruit route, that meant an orange Creamsicle with its electric orange shell and creamy, sweet filling. This pop is my attempt at re-creating my childhood favorite, avoiding whatever ingredients created the shocking orange color of the original and relying instead on whole foods and healthy ingredients. The result is a cool, creamy, sweet treat with nothing but good stuff involved.

1 cup coconut cream (from one 13.5-ounce can full-fat coconut milk)

1 cup plain whole milk yogurt

1 cup freshly squeezed orange juice (from 1 to 2 large oranges)

4 tablespoons honey

½ teaspoon pure vanilla extract

½ cup shredded unsweetened coconut, toasted (see page 24)

1   Chill a can of coconut milk undisturbed overnight so that the coconut cream separates from the coconut water. Carefully open the can and use a spoon to scoop out just the coconut cream, which will have risen to the top (reserve the remaining coconut water beneath for another use).

2   In a large glass measuring cup, combine the coconut cream, yogurt, orange juice, honey, and vanilla and whisk until well combined.

3   Pour the liquid into pop molds, insert sticks, and freeze for at least 3 to 4 hours, until hardened.

4   Once the pops are frozen and you're ready to serve, run the molds under hot water, loosening them up and melting the tips just a bit to help the toasted coconut adhere. Roll the tips of the pops in toasted coconut and serve.

VITAMIN C SOOTHER POPS v

Makes 10 pops

The worst colds are the ones that sneak up on you during the summer months. Winter colds are understandable; they're an unfortunate part of living in a frigid climate. But sniffling during the summer is just unfair. Fight off summer colds and general ickiness with these pops, which provide a huge (and delicious!) boost of vitamin C. This is one recipe where using a juicer is imperative, as blending and straining the ingredients will not give you the desired consistency.

2 large beets, trimmed, peeled, and roughly chopped

1-inch piece ginger, peeled and roughly chopped

2 oranges, peeled and roughly chopped

1 cup raspberries

3 carrots, peeled and roughly chopped

1 Press all the ingredients through a juicer and stir the juices until combined. Pour the liquid into pop molds, insert sticks, and freeze for at least 3 to 4 hours, until hardened.

PIÑA COLADA POPS v

Makes 10 pops

There are some flavors that seem as though they were born to be together; pineapple and coconut is one of those pairings. Like a classic piña colada, this pop relies on the sweetness of pineapple and the creaminess of coconut milk. Though you can buy pre-cut pineapple chunks if you are in a hurry, I highly recommend taking the time to skin, core, and slice a whole pineapple. This will result in a juicier, sweeter pop. If making these for the twenty-one–plus crowd, feel free to add a splash of rum for an authentic piña colada cocktail experience; if you do, keep your pops in the freezer for an additional 3 to 4 hours to harden.

1 medium pineapple, peeled, cored, and chopped, or 4 cups pre-cut pineapple

1 cup full-fat coconut milk (from one 13.5-ounce can)

1 teaspoon coconut sugar

¼ teaspoon pure vanilla extract

1 Add the pineapple to a blender with the coconut milk, coconut sugar, and vanilla and blend until well mixed. Pour the liquid into pop molds, insert sticks, and freeze for at least 3 to 4 hours, until hardened.

ALMOND BUTTER POPS WITH CHOCOLATE DRIZZLE

Makes 12 pops

Whole milk yogurt is sweetened with honey and bananas and flavored with almond butter to create the creamy base for these nutritious yet rich pops. The chocolate drizzle elevates the pops both aesthetically and in terms of richness. I like these pops topped with a sprinkle of toasted coconut, although toasted crushed nuts are also tasty.

⅓ cup creamy almond butter, homemade (page 30) or store-bought

½ cup plain whole milk yogurt

½ cup almond milk, homemade (page 29) or store-bought

2 frozen bananas

2 tablespoons honey

6 ounces dark chocolate, roughly chopped

¼ cup toasted coconut or nuts (page 24)

1 In a blender, combine the almond butter, yogurt, almond milk, bananas, and honey and blend until smooth.

2 Pour the mixture into pop molds, insert sticks, and freeze for at least 3 to 4 hours, until hardened. Once the pops are frozen, prepare the chocolate drizzle and topping.

3 Using a double boiler (or metal bowl held over a pan of simmering water), melt the dark chocolate, stirring constantly to avoid scorching. Once it is completely melted, remove from the heat and set aside.

4 Line a baking sheet with parchment paper. Pull your pops out of the freezer, run the molds under hot water, and pull out the pops. Lay the pops flat on the parchment paper and use a spoon to drizzle the chocolate over the pops. Moving quickly, before the chocolate hardens, sprinkle the crushed coconut or nuts over each pop. Give the chocolate a minute to set, then flip the pops and repeat. Place the baking sheet in the freezer to allow the chocolate to set for 5 to 10 minutes before serving. To store the pops, place them in a freezer-safe lidded glass container with a sheet of parchment between each layer of pops.

MEXICAN CHOCOLATE
FUDGE POPS

Makes 6 pops

While traditional fudge pops are extremely tasty, I find them a bit lacking given their single flavor profile. By adding a bit of cinnamon and cayenne pepper, these fudgy pops pack a whole lot of punch and offer a more complex, layered flavor experience, at once creamy and chocolaty, while still delivering a spicy heat. However, if you are serving these pops to young children, you might choose to skip the cayenne.

One 13.5-ounce can full-fat coconut milk

5 tablespoons unsweetened cocoa powder

4 tablespoons honey

½ avocado

1 teaspoon pure vanilla extract

½ teaspoon ground cinnamon

¼ teaspoon ground cayenne

¼ teaspoon salt

1 In a small saucepan, combine the coconut milk, cocoa powder, and honey. Place over medium-low heat and stir gently until the cocoa powder and honey are completely incorporated. Remove from the heat.

2 Pour the mixture into a blender, add the avocado, vanilla, cinnamon, cayenne, and salt and blend until smooth. Pour the liquid into the pop molds, insert sticks, and freeze for at least 3 to 4 hours, until hardened.

CREAMY CASHEW POPS WITH CHOCOLATE SHELL v

Makes 6 pops

A nod to traditional chocolate-covered ice cream bars, these pops instead rely on cashew cream for the filling. Dates, coconut butter, and vanilla extract add warmth and sweetness to the creamy middle, while chocolate mixed with coconut oil makes for a crunchy outer shell. I prefer rolling these in toasted chopped pecans, but you can experiment with finely chopped cacao nibs, toasted coconut, or roasted salted pistachios. You might even give the chocolate shell the slightest sprinkle of large flake sea salt.

1½ cups Cashew Cream
(page 27)

4 Medjool dates, pitted

1 teaspoon pure vanilla extract

1 tablespoon coconut butter

6 ounces dark chocolate,
roughly chopped

¼ cup coconut oil

¼ cup toasted and finely
chopped pecans (page 24)

1 In a blender, combine the cashew cream, dates, vanilla, and coconut butter and blend until smooth. Pour the mixture into pop molds, insert sticks, and place in the freezer for at least 3 to 4 hours, until hardened. Once the pops are hardened, prepare the chocolate shell and nut topping.

2 Using a double boiler (or metal bowl held over a pan of simmering water), melt the dark chocolate, stirring constantly to avoid scorching. Once melted, remove it from the heat, add the coconut oil, and stir until the oil is melted and well combined.

3 Line a baking sheet with parchment paper. Take your pops out of the freezer, run the molds under hot water, and pull out the pops. Lay the pops on the parchment paper and bring over the bowl of chocolate and toasted nuts.

4 Working one at a time, roll the pops in the chocolate, to thickly coat. The chocolate mixture will harden when it touches the cold pop. Dip it in the chocolate a few times to completely cover the pop. Last, dip the end of the pop into the chocolate once more, then quickly roll it in the nuts. Lay it on the parchment paper. Repeat for the rest of the pops. Place the baking sheet in the freezer to allow the chocolate to set for 5 to 10 minutes before serving. Store the pops in a freezer-safe lidded glass container with a sheet of parchment between each layer.

BANANA BITES v

Makes 20 bites

This frozen treat with just five ingredients is the epitome of simple. Bananas are sliced into rounds, then are dipped in chocolate and rolled in roasted, salted pecans for a creamy yet crunchy treat that satisfies both your sweet and salty cravings. For a more pop-like experience, you can cut each banana into three chunks and place them on skewers before rolling them in the chocolate and nuts. I prefer the bites because large hunks of banana tend to be pretty tough to bite when frozen solid.

½ cup pecans

1 tablespoon coconut oil, melted

½ teaspoon large flake sea salt

6 ounces dark chocolate, roughly chopped

2 bananas

1 Preheat the oven to 325°F.

2 In a small bowl, toss the pecans, coconut oil, and salt; mix well so that the pecans are evenly coated.

3 Lay the pecans in a single layer on a baking sheet and bake until they are fragrant and toasty in appearance, about 15 minutes. Remove from the oven and allow to cool, then chop the nuts into smaller pieces. (I like to place another sheet of parchment paper on top of the cooled nuts and use a rolling pin to break them up.)

4 Using a double boiler (or metal bowl held over a pan of simmering water), melt the chocolate, stirring constantly to avoid scorching. Once the chocolate is melted, remove it from the heat and set aside.

5 Cover a baking sheet with parchment paper. Peel the bananas and slice them into ½-inch-thick rounds.

6 Working with one piece at a time, dip a banana round into the chocolate, fully covering the surface, and then roll it around in the nuts (it helps to use a toothpick or skewer). Place it on the parchment paper and repeat for the remaining banana rounds. When finished, place the baking sheet in the freezer for 15 minutes to allow the chocolate to set. To store the banana bites, place them in a freezer-safe lidded glass container with a sheet of parchment between each layer of bites.

SNOW CONES, SLUSHIES, AND GRANITAS

SNOW CONES, SLUSHIES, AND GRANITAS fall under the same umbrella due to their icy consistency. Snow cones consist of shaved ice drizzled with flavored syrup. Slushies are simply flavored frozen drinks—a broad definition to be sure—but that pretty much sums it up; slushies tend to be a bit icier than their smoothie and shake counterparts. Finally, granitas are made by combining sweetener, flavoring, and water, and freezing until it reaches crystal form. The key to great snow cones, slushies, and granitas is to keep the icy consistency light and fluffy.

These treats are all incredibly light. They're the perfect end to an al fresco summer dinner, and the beauty with these desserts is that they let the fruit shine. Choosing fruit that is perfectly ripe, in season, and straight from the farm will ensure that your desserts are as flavorful as possible.

BLUEBERRY LEMONADE
SNOW CONES

Makes 1 cup syrup

Plump, sweet blueberries pair with tart lemonade in this refreshing syrup perfect for drizzling over shaved ice. First a blueberry sauce is made by simmering down berries with a dollop of honey; once strained, the rich blue liquid is added to freshly squeezed lemonade for a refreshing sweet-sour combination.

2 tablespoons water, divided
1 teaspoon arrowroot starch
2 cups blueberries
2 tablespoons honey
⅔ cup freshly squeezed lemon juice (from 3 to 4 lemons)
About 2 heaping cups shaved ice per person

1 In a small bowl, whisk together 1 tablespoon of the water and the arrowroot starch until dissolved. Set aside.

2 In a small saucepan, combine the blueberries, the remaining 1 tablespoon water, and the honey. Place over medium-low heat, bring to a simmer, and cook until the berries begin to soften and release their liquid, 5 to 7 minutes. Add the arrowroot slurry to the pan and stir to incorporate. Remove from the heat and allow to cool and thicken. Strain the syrup through a fine-mesh sieve into a bowl, pressing on the solids to make sure you extract all the berry juice. Compost the solids. Add the lemon juice to the syrup and stir.

3 Using a shaved ice machine, a hand ice shaver, or a blender, prepare your shaved ice.

4 For serving, add about 2 heaping cups of shaved ice to a small cup or paper cone and drizzle the syrup over the ice just enough to color it but not enough to melt the ice, about $1/3$ cup. Note the juice is quite strong on its own but works perfectly when drizzled over shaved ice.

5 Store the syrup in a glass bottle with a tight-fitting top. It will keep for up to 2 weeks in the refrigerator.

POMEGRANATE SNOW CONES

Makes 1 cup syrup

Extracting the juice from pomegranate seeds requires a bit of finesse, but it is quite easy once you get the hang of it, and it's worth the extra effort to experience its bright, tangy flavor. After extracting the juice, cook it down with a bit of honey and watch it turn into a gorgeous, ruby-hued syrup that is refreshingly simple and light when drizzled over shaved ice.

2 cups pomegranate seeds
(from 1 pomegranate)
1 tablespoon water
1 teaspoon arrowroot starch
1 tablespoon honey
About 2 heaping cups shaved
ice per person

1 Add the pomegranate seeds to a blender. Using the blender's pulse button, give the seeds a few pulses. You want the flesh to separate from the seeds, but you don't want to break apart the seeds. Pour the mixture through a fine-mesh sieve into a bowl, pushing the seeds hard to extract any last juices. Compost the solids.

2 In a small bowl, whisk together the water and arrowroot starch until dissolved. Set aside.

3 In a small saucepan, combine the pomegranate juice and honey. Place over medium heat, bring to a simmer, and cook, stirring until the honey is well incorporated, 2 to 4 minutes. Add the arrowroot slurry to the pan and stir to incorporate. Remove from the heat and allow the mixture to thicken as it cools.

4 Using a shaved ice machine, a hand ice shaver, or a blender, prepare your shaved ice.

5 For serving, add about 2 heaping cups of shaved ice to a small cup or paper cone and drizzle the syrup over the ice just enough to color it but not enough to melt the ice, about $1/3$ cup. Store the syrup in a glass bottle with a tight-fitting top. It will keep for up to 2 weeks in the refrigerator.

MANGO HONEY SNOW CONES

Makes 1 cup syrup

Mango pairs perfectly with a squeeze of orange juice to create a bright, sweet syrup. Picking a perfectly ripe, juicy mango is the key to achieving a sweet syrup. Ripe mangos will be slightly soft to the touch but not mushy enough to allow your fingers to sink into the skin, and they will have a sweet, fragrant, fruity smell near the stem. They should be full, plump, and shaped like a small football, and don't worry too much about color—there are over a thousand varieties of mango in the world, each with its own coloring.

1 mango, peeled, pitted, and chopped

½ cup freshly squeezed orange juice (from 1 orange)

1 tablespoon water

1 teaspoon arrowroot starch

1 tablespoon honey

About 2 heaping cups shaved ice per person

1　In a blender, combine the mango with the orange juice and blend until well mixed. Pour the mixture through a fine-mesh sieve into a bowl and allow the juice to separate. This will take some time—10 to 15 minutes—as the mixture will be thick. Compost the pulp.

2　In a small bowl, whisk together the water and arrowroot starch until dissolved. Set aside.

3　In a small saucepan, combine the mango juice and honey. Place over medium heat, bring to a simmer, and cook, stirring until the honey is well incorporated, 2 to 4 minutes. Add the arrowroot slurry to the pan and stir to incorporate. Remove from heat and allow the mixture to thicken as it cools.

4　Using a shaved ice machine, a hand ice shaver, or a blender, prepare your shaved ice.

5　For serving, add about 2 heaping cups of shaved ice to a small cup or paper cone and drizzle the syrup over the ice just enough to color it but not enough to melt the ice, about ⅓ cup. Store the syrup in a glass bottle with a tight-fitting top. It will keep for up to 2 weeks in the refrigerator.

TART CHERRY LIMEADE SLUSHIES

Serves 2

Having spent every summer in Northern Michigan, which is renowned for its cherry crop, I consider myself a bit of a cherry connoisseur. Driving along the country roads that surround my family's cottage, it's one cherry orchard after another, each with a handmade sign advertising buckets of both sweet dark cherries and tart cherries. I have yet to find tart cherries in the grocery stores of New England, but you can order them directly from orchards, such as King Orchards in Michigan, my personal favorite, which grows the Montmorency variety. It's worth the extra effort to experience the refreshing tartness and unique health benefits of these cherries. Montmorency cherries are one of the few known natural food sources of melatonin, which helps the body maintain healthy sleep cycles.

3 cups water

¼ cup honey, plus more for serving (optional)

1 cup freshly squeezed lime juice (from 4 to 5 limes)

1 teaspoon lime zest

1½ cups pitted frozen tart cherries

1 cup ice cubes

1 In a small saucepan, combine 2 cups of the water with the honey. Place over medium heat, bring to a simmer, and stir until the honey is completely dissolved. Remove from the heat and pour into a pitcher; add the lime juice and the remaining 1 cup water. Place the pitcher in the refrigerator and allow to cool for a couple hours, until completely chilled.

2 In a blender, combine the limeade with the lime zest, frozen cherries, and ice cubes and blend until frothy. Pour into two frosted glasses and serve, drizzled with a bit of honey if you find the slushie a bit tart for your liking.

PINEAPPLE MINT SLUSHIES v

Serves 2

Creamy and sweet with just a hint of mint, this refreshing slushie takes only seconds to whip up. I keep my freezer stocked with containers of frozen fruit so that whenever the urge strikes to whip up a slushie, shake, or smoothie, I'm ready to go. If you haven't prepped ahead, you can use fresh pineapple, though the resulting slushie will be considerably less frosty—but no less sweet!

¼ cup coconut cream (from one 13.5-ounce can full-fat coconut milk)

½ cup freshly squeezed orange juice (from 1 orange)

¼ cup shredded mint leaves, plus mint sprigs for serving

1 cup frozen pineapple chunks

1 cup ice cubes

1 Chill a can of coconut milk undisturbed overnight so that the coconut cream separates from the coconut water. Carefully open the can and use a spoon to scoop out just the coconut cream (reserve the remaining coconut water for another use).

2 Squeeze the orange juice into a glass measuring cup. Submerge the shredded mint leaves in the juice, muddle, then let sit for 15 minutes.

3 While juice is infusing, combine the pineapple chunks, coconut cream, and ice cubes in a blender and blend on high speed until frothy and well mixed. Strain the mint leaves from the orange juice, add the juice to the blender, and blend until combined.

4 Pour into two frosted glasses and garnish each with a sprig of mint.

STRAWBERRY RHUBARB GRANITA

Serves 6

The perfect spring pairing, strawberry and rhubarb make for a sweet yet tart, refreshing granita. Aim for just-picked, farm-fresh strawberries for maximum sweetness to counter the tart flavor of rhubarb.

1¼ cups water

1½ cups chopped rhubarb

1½ cups hulled and chopped strawberries

¼ cup honey

1 teaspoon lemon zest

⅓ cup freshly squeezed lemon juice (from 2 lemons)

Basil or mint sprigs for serving (optional)

1 Before beginning your recipe, place a 9 x 13-inch baking dish (preferably Pyrex or glass) in the freezer to chill for 1 hour.

2 In a medium saucepan, combine the water, rhubarb, strawberries, honey, and lemon zest. Place over medium heat, bring to a simmer, and cook until the mixture becomes soft, fragrant, and bubbly, about 6 minutes. Remove from the heat, pour the mixture through a fine-mesh sieve, and press out the juices. Compost the pulp. Allow the juice to cool, then add the lemon juice.

3 Pour into the chilled baking dish and freeze until the mixture becomes slushy, 30 to 45 minutes.

4 Rake the surface with a fork to break up the ice crystals—this is to prevent the juice from freezing into a hard block but rather small, delicate ice crystals. Repeat every 30 minutes, raking vigorously to break up the ice crystals, until all the juice is frozen, 3 to 4 more times. The whole process should take 2 to 3 hours. Scoop the granita into bowls and top with a basil or mint sprig if you like. You can store the granita in the freezer, covered in the baking dish, for up to 4 days, though the longer it stores, the harder it will freeze. Scrape it before serving.

APPLE SPICE GRANITA

Serves 6

Fall is synonymous with apple picking here in New England. Our favorite orchard is a short drive from our home and provides us with plentiful heirloom apple varieties for picking. By juicing your own apples, you can be assured that you're working with nothing but pure fruit juice, without any sweeteners or additives. Almost any apple variety will work here, though I prefer the sweetness of Jonagold or the juiciness of McIntosh. If you don't own a juicer, you can use store-bought apple juice, though you will want to look for unsweetened varieties. If the juice is sweetened, lessen or leave out the honey in the recipe.

6 to 8 apples, cored and chopped, or 3 cups apple juice

¼ cup honey

1 stick cinnamon

1 tablespoon freshly squeezed lemon juice

1　Before beginning your recipe, place a 9 x 13-inch baking dish (preferably Pyrex or glass) in the freezer to chill for 1 hour.

2　Push the apples through a juicer to make 3 cups.

3　In a small saucepan, combine the apple juice with the honey and cinnamon stick. Place over medium heat, bring to a simmer, and cook, stirring well to fully incorporate the honey, 3 to 5 minutes. Remove from the heat and allow the cinnamon to steep for 15 minutes while the mixture cools. Compost the cinnamon stick and stir in the lemon juice.

4　Pour into the chilled baking dish and freeze until the mixture becomes slushy, 30 to 45 minutes.

5　Rake the surface with a fork to break up the ice crystals—this is to prevent the juice from freezing into a hard block but rather small, delicate ice crystals. Repeat every 30 minutes, raking vigorously to break up the ice crystals, until all the juice is frozen, 3 to 4 more times. The whole process should take 2 to 3 hours. Scoop the granita into bowls and garnish with a stick of cinnamon. You can store the granita in the freezer, covered in the baking dish, for up to 4 days, though the longer it stores, the harder it will freeze. Scrape it before serving.

GRAPEFRUIT WITH
ELDERFLOWER CORDIAL GRANITA v

Serves 6

In Northern Michigan, where I spend my summers, elderflower grows with wild abundance. In the early summer months, I have a few secret spots where I go to forage. I'm willing to wade through bogs and even hurdle a beaver dam to reach the most prolific shrub. I bring home armfuls of the blooms and prepare them for a simple cordial. When making the cordial for this granita, I leave out sweetener because the granita itself has coconut sugar. If you're looking for the same flavor with less work, substitute 2 tablespoons St-Germain Elderflower Liqueur for the homemade cordial. An added bonus to using the liqueur: alcohol doesn't freeze, so it helps prevent the granita from getting an icy consistency.

12 elderflower heads, plus
5 sprigs for serving (optional)

2 tablespoons lemon zest
(from 1 to 2 lemons)

4 cups boiling water

2 cups freshly squeezed
grapefruit juice (from about
3 to 4 grapefruits)

¼ cup coconut sugar, plus
more for serving

1 Before beginning your recipe, place a 9 x 13-inch baking dish (preferably Pyrex or glass) in the freezer to chill for 1 hour.

2 For the cordial: Wash and inspect the elderflower heads, removing any brown flowers or insects. Place the flower heads in a large bowl and add the lemon zest. Pour 3 cups of the boiling water over the elderflowers, cover, and allow to infuse over-night. In the morning, pour the mixture through a fine-mesh sieve, and compost the solids. Your cordial is now ready for use.

3 For the granita: In a medium bowl, combine the grapefruit juice and coconut sugar with the remaining 1 cup boiling water and whisk until the sugar is dissolved. Add 2 tablespoons of the elderflower cordial and stir to combine. Place the

continued

GRAPEFRUIT WITH
ELDERFLOWER CORDIAL
GRANITA, continued

mixture in the chilled baking dish and freeze until the mixture becomes slushy, 30 to 45 minutes.

4 Rake the surface with a fork to break up the ice crystals—this is to prevent the juice from freezing into a hard block but rather small, delicate ice crystals. Repeat every 30 minutes, raking vigorously to break up the ice crystals, until all the juice is frozen, 3 to 4 more times. The whole process should take 2 to 3 hours. Scoop into bowls and top with a sprinkle of coconut sugar. You can store the granita in the freezer, covered in the baking dish, for up to 4 days, though the longer it stores, the harder it will freeze. Scrape it before serving.

FLAVORED ICE

AS A KID, I loved flavored ice pouches. I remember the excitement of snipping off the plastic top, pushing up the brightly dyed stick of ice, and slurping it down. As an adult, looking over the ingredient list leaves me feeling less than excited. But why not re-create these childhood favorites using real fruit? The flavor options are seemingly endless!

The easiest way to make flavored ice is by purchasing a plastic sleeve specifically designed for this purpose. I use Zipzicles. You can also use the flavored ice recipes as bases for ice pops. Simply pour them into your favorite pop molds, insert sticks, and allow them to freeze for 3 to 5 hours, until hardened. These recipes tend to be a bit more watery than the pop recipes, and the melted juice is meant to be slurped from the flavored ice tubes, so don't be surprised if your pops melt quickly.

STRAWBERRY LEMONADE ICE

Makes 6 flavored ices

Lemonade is the quintessential drink of summer, and it just so happens that when paired with bright swirls of strawberry puree, it becomes even sweeter. I love the way the sourness of the lemon plays with the sweetness of strawberries, but if the lemonade mixture tastes too sour for your liking, feel free to add a bit more honey before distributing into the flavored ice pouches.

¼ cup water

2 cups hulled and chopped strawberries

1 tablespoon honey

4 tablespoons freshly squeezed lemon juice (from 1 to 2 lemons)

1 teaspoon lemon zest (from about 1 lemon)

1 In a small saucepan, combine the water, strawberries, and honey. Place over medium heat, bring to a simmer, and cook, stirring frequently, until the mixture becomes fragrant and the berries begin to soften and give off their juices, 5 to 8 minutes. Remove from the heat and allow the mixture to cool and thicken.

2 Pour the berries and their juices into a blender and add the lemon juice and zest. Blend until well combined.

3 Using a funnel or turkey baster, fill individual ice pouches. Seal and freeze for at least 3 to 4 hours before enjoying.

COCONUT NECTARINE ICE v

Makes 4 flavored ices

Nectarines have a natural juiciness that pairs well with the creaminess of coconut milk. The coconut milk helps to cut the tartness from the nectarines, leaving you with a silky smooth puree that is nothing but sweet. It's important to choose ripe, juicy nectarines, the kind that give a bit when you squeeze them.

3 nectarines, peeled, halved, and pitted

3 tablespoons full-fat coconut milk (from one 13.5-ounce can)

1 In a blender, combine the nectarines with the coconut milk and blend until smooth.

2 Using a funnel or turkey baster, fill individual ice pouches. Seal and freeze for at least 3 to 4 hours before enjoying.

HONEY POACHED PLUM ICE

Makes 6 flavored ices

Bushels of plums begin to appear at my farmers' market in late July and tend to stick around through the fall. It's hard not to be entranced by their deep purple skin, though I often find the Mirabelle plum, a golden yellow variety, to be equally sweet and juicy. When choosing plums, make sure to give them a gentle squeeze. The flesh should give slightly under your fingertips, letting you know that the plum is ripe and juicy. Poaching plums softens the flesh and intensifies the sweetness. The skin falls away easily after poaching, leaving you with just the poaching syrup and flesh. A quick whirl in the blender produces a rich, sweet puree that is perfect for turning into flavored ice.

3 plums
2 cups water
2 tablespoons honey

1 With a sharp knife, lightly score the plums all the way around, starting and ending at the stem, and slicing just through the skin.

2 In a medium saucepan, bring the water to a boil over high heat. Add the honey and stir until it's dissolved. Place the plums in the pan, reduce the heat to medium-low, and simmer until the plums are just tender, 15 to 20 minutes. Remove the pan from the heat and let the plums cool in the poaching liquid.

3 Once the plums are cool enough to handle, strip away the skin and take out the pits. Place the plums and their poaching liquid in a blender and puree.

4 Using a funnel or turkey baster, fill individual ice pouches. Seal and freeze for at least 3 to 4 hours before enjoying.

VANILLA ROASTED APRICOT ICE

Makes 6 flavored ices

Roasting apricot with vanilla bean lends an incredible warmth and richness to the fruit. Roasting also intensifies the sweetness and softens the flesh of the apricots, making them ideal for pureeing.

·¼ cup water
1 tablespoon honey
1 tablespoon coconut oil
1 vanilla bean
4 apricots, halved and pitted

1 Preheat the oven to 400°F.

2 In a shallow baking dish, combine the water, honey, and coconut oil. Slice the vanilla bean lengthwise, scrape the seeds into the baking dish, then add the bean. Place the apricots flesh side up in the baking dish and roast until they are tender, 12 to 14 minutes. Allow the apricots to cool in their juices, then remove and compost the vanilla bean.

3 Place the apricots and their roasting juices in a blender and puree.

4 Using a funnel or turkey baster, fill individual ice pouches. Seal and freeze for at least 3 to 4 hours before enjoying.

HONEYDEW MINT ICE v

Makes 6 flavored ices

Honeydew and mint are a natural pair. Honeydew has a soft, subtle sweetness, and mint helps to punch up the flavor. Feel free to play with the mint proportions; if you are serving these to adults, double up on the mint and add a splash of rum for a mojito-inspired frozen treat.

3 cups chopped honeydew melon

2 tablespoons freshly squeezed lime juice (from 1 lime)

¼ cup mint leaves

1 In a blender, combine the honeydew, lime juice, and mint leaves and blend until well mixed. Pour the mixture through a fine-mesh sieve into a bowl and compost the solids.

2 Using a funnel or turkey baster, fill individual ice pouches. Seal and freeze for at least 3 to 4 hours before enjoying.

WATERMELON LIME ICE v

Makes 6 flavored ices

In-season, farm-fresh watermelon is sweet enough on its own, no need to add anything but a squeeze of lime and a bit of zest for kick. Simple, summery goodness! If you're serving this to an adult crowd, consider adding a splash of tequila for a margarita-like frozen treat.

2 cups seeded and chopped watermelon

2 tablespoons freshly squeezed lime juice (from 1 lime)

1 teaspoon lime zest (from 1 lime)

1 In a blender, combine the watermelon, lime juice, and lime zest and blend until well mixed. If you prefer a smoother pop, pour the mixture through a fine-mesh sieve into a bowl and compost the solids; I prefer to skip the straining.

2 Using a funnel or turkey baster, fill individual ice pouches. Seal and freeze for at least 3 to 4 hours before enjoying.

PASSION FRUIT PINEAPPLE ICE v

Makes 6 flavored ices

Passion fruit is a tropical fruit with an exotic-looking interior. Beneath its lackluster peel lie small black seeds surrounded by incredibly tart-flavored fruit. The seeds are edible and give this flavored ice an unexpected crunch. Pairing the passion fruit with a base of pineapple makes for a tropically flavored treat that is as sweet as it is tart.

2 cups peeled, cored, and chopped pineapple
2 passion fruits, sliced in half

1 In a blender, blend the pineapple chunks until smooth. Pour the mixture through a fine-mesh sieve set over a pitcher and compost the solids.

2 With a spoon, gently scrape the passion fruit insides (seeds and all) into the pitcher with the pineapple, and give it a gentle stir. Be careful to scoop out just the flesh of the passion fruit— the white skin of the rind is bitter in flavor, and you should be careful to avoid it during scooping.

3 Using a funnel or turkey baster (making sure the opening is large enough for the passion fruit seeds to pass through), fill individual ice pouches. Seal and freeze for at least 3 to 4 hours before enjoying.

KIWI PINEAPPLE ICE

Makes 5 flavored ices

Kiwis, with their beautiful, speckled flesh, have a slightly sour flavor, but when paired with sweet, juicy pineapple, the overall effect is wonderfully tropical. When blending, take extra care not to break up the kiwi seeds, which can lend a bitter flavor to the mixture; I use the pulse button on my blender to help avoid overblending. If you'd prefer a flavored ice without the seeds, simply pour the blended mixture through a fine-mesh sieve. I personally like the look of the seeds, and they don't alter the flavor in any way when whole.

4 kiwis, peeled and roughly chopped

1 cup peeled, cored, and chopped pineapple

1 teaspoon honey

1 In a blender, combine the kiwi, pineapple, and honey and blend on a low speed or using the pulse button, being careful not to overblend and break up the kiwi seeds.

2 Using a funnel or turkey baster, fill individual ice pouches. Seal and freeze for at least 3 to 4 hours before enjoying.

POACHED PEAR
WITH THYME ICE

Makes 6 flavored ices

Poaching is a gentle method for increasing the sweetness of pears. For this particular recipe, I like Barlett pears, which become very soft and almost fall apart in the poaching process. You can also try Bosc, Comice, or Forelle varieties. Make sure your pears are ripe but still firm. Once the pears have become overripe and a bit mushy, they won't hold up when poached.

3 cups water
4 tablespoons honey
2 sprigs thyme
3 pears, peeled

1 In a large saucepan, combine the water and honey. Place over medium heat, bring to a simmer, and cook, stirring, until the honey is dissolved. Add the thyme and the pears and reduce the heat to medium-low. Keeping the liquid at a very low simmer, poach the pears for 15 minutes, or until fragrant and soft. Remove from heat and allow to cool.

2 Once the pears are cool enough to handle, remove their cores. Remove the thyme from the poaching liquid and compost it.

3 In a blender, combine the pear slices and their poaching liquid and blend until well mixed. Pour the mixture through a fine-mesh sieve and compost the solids.

4 Using a funnel or turkey baster, fill individual ice pouches. Seal and freeze for at least 3 to 4 hours before enjoying.

FROZEN YOGURT AND SORBET

ALTHOUGH THE TERM "FROZEN YOGURT" refers to yogurt that is flavored, sweetened, and frozen, I've taken a more liberal approach to the definition. For the sake of this book, frozen yogurt is the category of creamy, frozen treats that are lighter than ice cream but contain a creaminess you won't find in the icier desserts like slushies and granitas. A few of the following recipes rely on bananas to achieve their creamy consistency, while others indeed live up to their name and use yogurt as the base.

Store-bought frozen yogurt is often scoopable the moment you pull it out of the freezer, thanks to the addition of stabilizers as well as the commercial churning process. You will find that these frozen yogurt recipes will require twenty to thirty minutes of thawing before they are soft and creamy enough to scoop. I strongly recommend serving the frozen yogurt directly from the ice cream maker for the softest, creamiest results. The consistency will be similar to soft serve yogurt, and it will be delicious.

You'll also find three sorbet recipes included in this section. Sorbet is defined simply as a dairy-free dessert made from sweetened water that has been flavored and churned. The result is a dense, flavorful creation that lacks any fat. While the flavor possibilities are endless—and most of us have enjoyed common favorites such as watermelon, strawberry, peach, and raspberry—I've chosen to focus on three sorbets that are a bit surprising and wholly original.

Sorbet becomes very hard when frozen because of its lack of fat, though the addition of arrowroot starch helps give it softness and scoopability. I prefer to serve my sorbet directly from the ice cream machine; for slightly firmer scoops, freeze it for an hour after it churns. If you need to freeze the sorbet for any length of time, give it ten to fifteen minutes to soften out of the freezer before serving. For a softer, easier-to-scoop end result, many sorbet recipes call for alcohol. Since alcohol doesn't freeze, it makes for a softer sorbet and, indeed, any of the recipes here would taste wonderful with a tablespoon or two of alcohol added: Concord Grape Sorbet (page 127) would taste amazing with a splash of rosé and Blood Orange Sorbet (page 128) would do nicely with a shot of gin.

Traditional sorbet recipes rely on refined white sugar for their sweetness, but I find that using honey or other natural sweeteners works just fine. It may not follow tradition, but the results are just as sweet and the fruit is really allowed to shine.

ROASTED STRAWBERRY FROZEN YOGURT DOTS

Makes 10 to 12 strips

Do you remember those candy buttons that came on long paper strips? I'm pretty sure they were nothing but pure sugar with a bit of dye added for the neon pink, blue, and yellow colors. These frozen yogurt dots are a nod to those classic candies, though the ingredient list is much more desirable. My boys love getting their own strip of paper, peeling off the dots, and popping them in their mouths. They melt quickly on hot days, so you might want to take this treat outside to avoid a sticky mess!

1 pound strawberries, hulled and chopped

2 tablespoons honey

¼ teaspoon salt

1 teaspoon pure vanilla extract

1 cup plain whole milk yogurt

1 Preheat the oven to 375°F.

2 In a 9 x 13-inch baking dish, toss together the chopped strawberries, honey, salt, and vanilla. Roast until the juices are bubbling, 15 to 20 minutes. Remove from the oven and let cool to room temperature.

3 In a blender, combine the roasted strawberries and yogurt and blend until smooth. Pour the mixture into a freezer-safe container and chill for 1 hour in the freezer.

4 Line a baking sheet with parchment paper. Once the mixture has reached a thick, mostly frozen consistency, pour it into a pastry tube and squeeze small dots (slightly smaller than a dime) in lines on the parchment paper. Work quickly, because once the mixture thaws, it will become too runny to hold its shape.

5 When the parchment paper is full, place it in the freezer for 2 hours. Once completely frozen, the yogurt dots can be scraped off the paper and stored in a freezer-safe container; or cut the parchment into strips, loosely roll them up, and store them in a freezer-safe container.

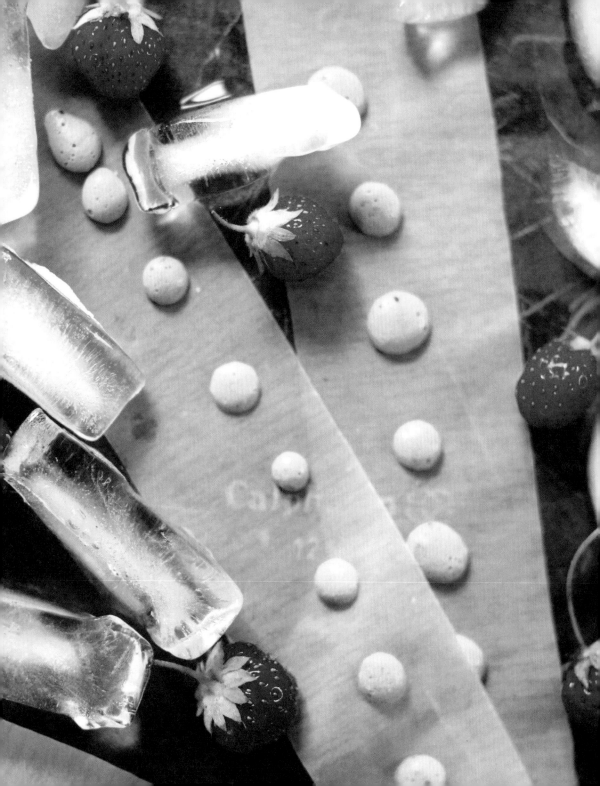

BERRY, LIME, AND COCONUT BUTTERMILK FROZEN YOGURT

Makes 2 pints

The combination of raspberries, coconut, and lime with the tanginess of whole milk yogurt and buttermilk makes for an incredibly light, rosy-hued treat. The bright sweetness of raspberries pairs nicely with the warmth and crunch of toasted coconut, while lime juice gives the whole thing a kick.

1 cup raspberries

¾ cup honey

1 teaspoon pure vanilla extract

¼ cup water

¼ teaspoon salt

⅓ cup shredded unsweetened coconut, toasted (see page 24)

2 cups plain whole milk yogurt

1 cup buttermilk

1 cup freshly squeezed lime juice (from 2 to 4 limes)

1　In a large saucepan, combine the raspberries, honey, vanilla, water, and salt. Place over medium heat and cook, stirring gently until the honey is dissolved and the berries have softened and given off some of their juices, 5 to 8 minutes. Remove the pan from the heat and allow to cool.

2　Transfer to a bowl and mix in the coconut, yogurt, buttermilk, and lime juice. Cover and place the bowl in the refrigerator for a few hours to chill thoroughly.

3　Freeze the mixture in an ice cream maker according to the manufacturer's instructions. You can eat the frozen yogurt right away for a softer version, or freeze it for about 2 hours for a firmer consistency.

BLACK CHERRY AND DARK CHOCOLATE CHUNK FROZEN "YOGURT" ᵥ

Makes 1 pint

Using bananas as the base for this frozen "yogurt" means a dairy-free creation that is still as creamy as its name suggests, and luscious black cherries and dark chocolate make for a sophisticated flavor combination. If you have this frozen treat on the menu, plan ahead and put your can of coconut milk in the refrigerator the night before so the cream separates from the water.

2 tablespoons coconut cream, plus more if needed (from one 13.5-ounce can full-fat coconut milk)

2 bananas

1½ cups pitted and chopped black cherries, divided

3 ounces Maple-Sweetened Chocolate (page 19) or other dark chocolate, roughly chopped

1 Chill a can of coconut milk undisturbed overnight so that the coconut cream separates from the coconut water. Carefully open the can and use a spoon to scoop out just the coconut cream (reserve the remaining coconut water for another use).

2 Place the bananas, 1 cup of the black cherries, and the coconut cream in a blender and blend until smooth, scraping down the sides as you blend and adding a little more coconut cream if needed to blend smoothly.

3 Scrape the mixture into a bowl and stir in the remaining 1/2 cup black cherries. Cover and place the bowl in the refrigerator to chill thoroughly.

4 Freeze the mixture in an ice cream maker according to the manufacturer's instructions, adding the chocolate during the final 5 minutes of churning. It's best to serve this frozen "yogurt" immediately; because of the small amount of fat and the water content of the bananas, it will get very hard when frozen for any length of time. If you do need to freeze it after churning, allow it to soften out of the freezer for at least 20 minutes before serving; it may appear a tad watery after thawing.

FROZEN YOGURT BARK

Makes 10 to 15 pieces of bark

This bark is a take on traditional chocolate bark, and it works perfectly as a fun-size frozen treat. The yogurt base is simple—plain whole milk yogurt sweetened with a bit of honey and a dash of vanilla extract—and from there this recipe is open for experimentation. You can simply throw in a couple cups of berries or chopped peaches, or you can get fancy, combining fruits, even adding nuts, chocolate chips, or seeds for crunch. Just be sure the mixture is spreadable— that's the key!

2 cups plain whole milk yogurt

⅓ cup honey

½ teaspoon pure vanilla extract

¼ teaspoon salt

2 cups fruit of your choice (such as blueberries, strawberries, cherries, raspberries, chopped peaches)

1 In a large bowl, whisk together the yogurt, honey, vanilla, and salt.

2 If the fruit you're using is large and has pits or stems (such as strawberries, cherries, or peaches), prepare the fruit by pitting/hulling/peeling and roughly chopping it. Raspberries and blueberries can be used whole. Gently stir the fruit into the yogurt mixture until just combined.

3 Pour the yogurt onto a baking sheet lined with parchment paper, using a spatula to spread it out smoothly and evenly. Give the fruit a bit of a press with the spatula to even out the surface. Freeze the baking sheet overnight and, when ready to serve, cut or break the sheet of yogurt into pieces. Store the yogurt bark in a lidded freezer-safe glass container with the layers of bark separated by parchment paper in the freezer for up to 2 weeks.

VANILLA BEAN FROZEN YOGURT

Makes 2 pints

It's nice to have a simple vanilla frozen yogurt recipe. Whether serving a slice of fruit pie à la mode or creating the perfect brownie sundae, vanilla yogurt can be just the thing. Because of its simple flavor profile, this frozen treat lends itself well to a playful assortment of toppings. I like a bit of crunch, so I load mine with toasted coconut, toasted chopped pecans, and cacao nibs. If I'm feeling extra decadent, I'll drizzle a hefty spoonful of Vegan Salted Caramel Sauce (page 186) on top. I let my boys eat this fro-yo for breakfast topped with chopped nuts and a sprinkle of toasted coconut or a handful of berries in the summer months. They think they're getting away with something, but really we're just talking about eating slightly sweetened yogurt here!

½ cup whole milk
1 vanilla bean
⅓ cup honey
2 cups plain whole milk yogurt
¼ teaspoon salt

1 Pour the milk into a small saucepan. Slice the vanilla bean lengthwise, scrape the seeds into the milk, then add the bean. Place over medium heat, bring to a simmer, stirring to avoid scalding the milk, then add the honey and simmer, stirring until the honey is well incorporated, 3 to 5 minutes. Remove the pan from heat and allow to cool, then remove and compost the vanilla bean.

2 In a large bowl, combine the milk mixture with the yogurt and salt. Cover and place the bowl in the refrigerator for a few hours to chill thoroughly.

3 Freeze the mixture in an ice cream maker according to the manufacturer's instructions. You can eat the frozen yogurt right away for a softer version, or freeze it for about 2 hours for a firmer consistency. When served right from the ice cream mixer, the frozen yogurt closely mimics the consistency of soft serve ice cream.

COFFEE FROZEN YOGURT

Makes 1 pint

I love a strong, dark cup of coffee, taken black with no cream or sugar. I prefer the same intensity when it comes to my coffee frozen yogurt. However, if you prefer a mellow coffee experience, you can scale the coffee back to 1/2 cup. Experiment to find your ideal coffee strength. Just make sure that you pick a blend with rich, full flavor. The flavor of the coffee can make or break this recipe—so brew a cup of your best beans. If you love the taste of espresso, you can substitute a double shot of espresso for the coffee for an incredibly rich, strong espresso frozen yogurt.

½ cup whole milk
2 tablespoons maple syrup
½ teaspoon salt
¾ cup strong brewed coffee
1 cup plain whole milk yogurt

1 In a small saucepan, combine the milk, maple syrup, and salt. Place over medium heat, bring to a simmer, and cook, stirring occasionally, for 3 to 5 minutes. Remove the pan from the heat and stir in the coffee. Allow the mixture to cool.

2 In a large bowl, combine the coffee mixture with the yogurt. Cover, and place the bowl in the refrigerator for a few hours to chill thoroughly.

3 Freeze the mixture in an ice cream maker according to the manufacturer's instructions. You can eat the frozen yogurt right away for a softer version, or freeze it for about 2 hours for a firmer consistency.

PUMPKIN FROZEN YOGURT WITH CANDIED PECANS

Makes 2 pints

Many a fall day here in New England could fool you into believing it's still summer. When warm sun rays combine with the crisp autumn air and changing leaves, the feeling is unbeatable. Celebrate those sunny fall days with a decidedly autumn-inspired frozen yogurt. I highly recommend roasting your own sugar pumpkin, but in a pinch, canned pumpkin will do just fine.

1 small sugar pumpkin (or one 15-ounce can pumpkin)

2 tablespoons olive oil

2 teaspoons ground cinnamon, divided

½ teaspoon freshly grated nutmeg

2 cups plain whole milk yogurt

¼ teaspoon ground ginger

⅔ cup plus 1 tablespoon maple syrup, divided

1 tablespoon coconut oil

1 cup pecans

1 To roast the pumpkin: Preheat the oven to 375°F and rub a baking sheet with the olive oil. Cut off the stem of the pumpkin, then slice it in half around the middle. Using a large spoon, remove the seeds and membranes and compost them (or save the seeds for making homemade roasted pumpkin seeds). Sprinkle the pumpkin flesh with 1 teaspoon of the cinnamon and ¼ teaspoon of the nutmeg. Place the pumpkin halves skin side up on the oiled baking sheet and roast for about 1 hour, until the pumpkin pierces easily with a fork. Leave the oven on.

2 Remove the pumpkin from the oven and allow it to cool until cool enough to handle. Scoop the pumpkin flesh into a blender, composting the skin, and blend until smooth.

3 In a large bowl, combine the yogurt, 1 cup of the pumpkin puree, the remaining 1 teaspoon cinnamon, the remaining ¼ teaspoon nutmeg, the ginger, and ⅔ cup of the maple syrup. Stir well, cover, and place the bowl in the refrigerator to chill thoroughly. Any leftover pumpkin puree can be used for baking, in soups, or even sweetened with maple syrup and stirred into oatmeal.

4 While the yogurt mixture is chilling, roast and candy the pecans: In a small saucepan, combine

continued

PUMPKIN
FROZEN YOGURT
WITH CANDIED
PECANS, continued

the remaining 1 tablespoon maple syrup with the coconut oil. Place over medium heat and cook, stirring, until the oil is melted. Then remove the pan from the heat and add the pecans, tossing until they are well coated. Spread the nuts out onto a baking sheet lined with parchment paper in a single layer, making sure they are not touching, and roast for 5 minutes. Remove from the oven and allow the nuts to cool on the baking sheet.

5 Freeze the mixture in an ice cream maker according to the manufacturer's instructions. Serve immediately for a soft serve version, or freeze for about 2 hours for a firmer consistency. Serve with a generous sprinkle of candied pecans.

CARAMELIZED ROASTED BANANA FROZEN "YOGURT" v

Makes 1 pint

This is such a simple, healthy frozen treat, and the creaminess can't be beat. The flavor of the roasted bananas is surprisingly rich, thanks to the maple syrup, which caramelizes nicely at high heat. When you transfer the caramelized bananas from the baking sheet into the blender, make sure to scrape every last crispy maple syrup bit into the mix.

4 overly ripe bananas

2 tablespoons coconut oil, melted

2 tablespoons maple syrup

⅛ teaspoon salt

¼ teaspoon ground cinnamon

¼ cup almond milk, homemade (page 29) or store-bought, plus more if needed

1 Preheat the oven to 400°F. Line a baking sheet with parchment paper.

2 Peel the bananas, then slice them into rounds. Place them in a bowl with the coconut oil, maple syrup, salt, and cinnamon and toss them until they are evenly coated. Spread the coated banana slices on the prepared baking sheet in a single layer, place them in the oven, and roast for 20 minutes, or until they have turned brown and the maple syrup is caramelizing. Be careful not to let the syrup burn—the sugars can quickly go from a toasty brown caramel to blackened. Remove from the oven and allow the bananas to cool.

3 Scrape the bananas and caramelizing liquid into the blender, add the almond milk, and blend until the mixture is smooth and creamy, streaming in a bit more almond milk if needed. Pour the mixture into a bowl, cover, and place it in the refrigerator for a few hours to chill thoroughly.

4 Freeze the mixture in an ice cream maker according to the manufacturer's instructions. It's best to serve this frozen "yogurt" immediately. Because of the lack of fat and the water content of the bananas, this treat will get very hard when frozen for any length of time. If you do need to freeze it after churning, allow it to soften out of the freezer for at least 20 minutes before serving.

BLACKBERRY TARRAGON SORBET

Makes 1 pint

Tarragon is an herb with a distinct anise flavor along with notes of pepper and pine, which play well against the sweetness of honey and tartness of blackberries. Be aware that tarragon is a strong herb and can easily dominate this dessert if you oversteep. This is a sophisticated-tasting sorbet, and its rich plum color would make it especially elegant if served in a champagne glass with a splash of bubbly.

½ cup water
2 cups blackberries
⅓ cup honey
1 sprig tarragon
1 teaspoon arrowroot starch

1 In a small saucepan, combine the water and blackberries, place over medium heat, and bring to a simmer, stirring gently until the berries begin to soften and release their juices. Begin mashing the berries with a fork or potato masher until they are nicely broken down, then remove them from the heat and press them through a fine-mesh sieve into a bowl. Compost the solids.

2 Return the juice to the pan, add the honey, and heat over medium heat, stirring, until the honey is dissolved. Remove from the heat, add the tarragon, cover the pan, and allow the tarragon to steep for 15 minutes. Remove and compost the tarragon and allow the mixture to cool. Ladle 1 tablespoon of the cooled liquid into a small bowl along with the arrowroot starch, whisking well. Add the arrowroot slurry back into the base and mix to incorporate.

3 Place the mixture in a bowl, cover it, and allow it to chill thoroughly in the refrigerator for a few hours.

4 Freeze the blackberry mixture in an ice cream maker according to the manufacturer's instructions. Serve immediately for a soft serve version, or freeze for about 2 hours for a firmer consistency.

CONCORD GRAPE SORBET

Makes 1 pint

Concord grapes can be found at farmers' markets come late fall. They're a sweet grape with large, crunchy seeds and slightly sour skin. The flavor of these grapes is often mimicked in grape-flavored juices and jellies, though if you've ever tasted the real thing, you'll know how much juicier and sweeter they are compared to imitations. If you're serving this to an adult crowd, consider adding a tablespoon or two of rosé to the base, which will give the sorbet a softer, more scoopable consistency.

¼ cup water

2 pounds Concord grapes, stems removed

⅓ cup honey

1 tablespoon freshly squeezed lemon juice

1 teaspoon arrowroot starch

1 In a small saucepan, combine the grapes and water. Place over medium heat and heat until the grapes release their juices, about 7 minutes, stirring gently to separate the grapes from their skins and break up the seeds and flesh. Remove the pan from the heat and strain the mixture through a fine-mesh sieve. Compost the solids.

2 Return the juice to saucepan, add the honey, and cook over medium heat, stirring, until the honey is dissolved. Remove from the heat, add the lemon juice, and allow the mixture to cool. Ladle 1 tablespoon of the cooled liquid into a small bowl along with the arrowroot starch and whisk well. Add the arrowroot slurry back into the base and mix to incorporate.

3 Pour the juice into a bowl, cover it, and place it in the refrigerator to chill thoroughly for a few hours.

4 Freeze the grape mixture in an ice cream maker according to the manufacturer's instructions. Serve immediately for a softer version, or freeze for about 2 hours for a firmer consistency.

BLOOD ORANGE SORBET

Makes 1 pint

Blood oranges, with their brilliant ruby flesh, are a winter crop available approximately from December through March (though this can vary slightly depending on the variety). Packed with vitamin C and rich in antioxidants, blood oranges are a great health booster during the cold months. One pound of fruit, or about three medium oranges, will give you approximately one cup of juice, so you'll need a hefty haul for this sorbet. There are citrus groves in California, Florida, and Texas that ship boxes of farm-fresh oranges, which is something to think about if you fall for this frosty, bright, immune-boosting sorbet. A tablespoon or two of gin added to the base would be a welcome addition to this vibrant sorbet if serving to an adult crowd.

1 cup water, divided
1 teaspoon arrowroot starch
¼ cup honey
3 cups freshly squeezed blood orange juice (from 10 to 12 blood oranges)
2 tablespoons freshly squeezed lemon juice

1 In a small bowl, mix 1 tablespoon of the water with the arrowroot starch. Set aside.

2 In a small saucepan, combine the remaining water and the honey. Place over medium heat, bring to a simmer, and stir until the honey is dissolved into the water. Add the arrowroot slurry mixture to the pan and stir to incorporate. Remove from the heat and pour the syrup into a pitcher or bowl.

3 Add the blood orange juice and lemon juice to the pitcher and stir to combine. Place the pitcher in the refrigerator and allow to cool for several hours, until completely chilled.

4 Freeze the blood orange mixture in an ice cream maker according to the manufacturer's instructions. Serve immediately for a soft serve version, or freeze for about 2 hours for a firmer consistency.

DAIRY-FREE
ICE CREAM

TRADITIONAL ICE CREAM BASES include ingredients such as cream, eggs, and sometimes even cream cheese. I just didn't feel right including those three ingredients in a recipe book that touted itself as healthy, and so I set about creating a base that still tasted creamy and decadent but lacked the heaviness of traditional ice cream. Enter cashew cream—an absolute dream ingredient for anyone who is attempting to make sweet, rich treats using non-dairy ingredients. When soaked overnight and blended with water, cashews turn into an incredibly rich, cream-like liquid. Using this cream plus coconut milk, I created a creamy ice cream base that doesn't require the usual slew of dairy products. The addition of arrowroot powder helps prevent ice crystals forming, which keeps the ice cream from becoming rock hard in your freezer. As an added bonus, you won't find yourself sweating over a hot stove attempting to stir your way to a perfect custard as is the case with traditional ice cream recipes.

An important note: most commercial ice creams are soft and scoopable almost immediately when you take them out of the refrigerator. There are many reasons why this is the case, including the addition of stabilizers and the fact that commercial ice cream machines churn more air into the ice cream than home ice cream machines do. Since the following ice cream recipes are lower in fat than traditional recipes and don't include stabilizers, the ice cream will be hard when you pull it from the freezer. Allowing the ice cream to thaw for 10 to 15 minutes will return it to its creamy state, but I highly recommend serving the ice cream directly from the machine for the creamiest consistency. I often make the ice cream base a day or two before I want to serve the ice cream, and then while we're eating dinner, I'll pour the base into the ice cream machine and let it churn for twenty to thirty minutes. This works perfectly: as we're clearing away the dinner plates, dessert is ready to go!

A final thought: if you plan on serving your ice cream to an adult-only crowd, you may experiment with adding a splash of alcohol to the base. Alcohol doesn't freeze, so it helps the ice cream maintain a softer consistency. If you don't want the alcohol to alter the ice cream's flavor, consider adding a tablespoon of vodka, which is rendered tasteless after the freezing and churning process. If you want the alcohol to play along with the ice cream, consider how the flavors might work together; for example, a tablespoon or two of rum would work perfectly with the Maple Pecan Crunch Ice Cream recipe (page 142).

RASPBERRY ICE CREAM WITH DARK CHOCOLATE

Makes 1 pint

Sweet, plump, in-season raspberries give this ice cream a gorgeous pink hue and juicy sweetness. I prefer using my favorite bar of dark chocolate and chopping it roughly with a large knife to achieve a mix of larger chunks and small nibs; this ensures that there is chocolate swirled throughout the mixture and in every bite.

1½ cups fresh raspberries

1 tablespoon freshly squeezed lemon juice

1½ cups full-fat coconut milk, divided (from one 13.5-ounce can)

1 tablespoon arrowroot starch

1 teaspoon pure vanilla extract

¼ teaspoon salt

½ cup honey

1 cup Cashew Cream (page 27)

3 ounces Maple-Sweetened Chocolate (page 19) or other dark chocolate, roughly chopped

1 Thoroughly rinse and dry the raspberries and place them in a large bowl. Using a fork, mash the berries until they are broken up and release their juices. Add the lemon juice and mix to incorporate.

2 Pour 2 tablespoons of the coconut milk into a small bowl, add the arrowroot starch, and whisk until dissolved. In a small saucepan, combine the arrowroot slurry, the remaining coconut milk, the vanilla, salt, and honey. Place over low heat, bring to a simmer, and cook, stirring, until the honey is dissolved into the coconut milk, 3 to 5 minutes. Remove the pan from the heat and allow the mixture to cool.

3 Add the coconut milk mixture to the bowl of raspberries, then incorporate the cashew cream, mixing well. Cover the mixture and chill in the refrigerator for a few hours.

4 Freeze in an ice cream maker according to the manufacturer's instructions, adding the chocolate to the machine during the final 5 minutes of churning. You can eat the ice cream right away for a softer version, or freeze it for about 2 hours for a firmer consistency.

KEY LIME PIE ICE CREAM

Makes 1 pint

Traditional Key lime desserts, including Key lime pie and ice cream, call specifically for Key limes, which have a stronger aroma, thinner peel, and a more tart flavor than the more commonly found Persian lime. If you can find Key limes, lucky you! You must be living in a warmer climate, most likely Florida, and for that, I envy you. For the rest of us, regular ole Persian limes, the ones you find at every grocery store, will work just fine.

1 cup full-fat coconut milk, divided (from one 13.5-ounce can)

1 tablespoon arrowroot starch

½ cup lime juice

1 tablespoon lime zest

½ cup honey

¼ teaspoon salt

1 cup Cashew Cream (page 27)

½ cup loosely packed spinach (optional, for color)

½ cup crushed graham crackers, homemade (page 157) or store-bought

1 Pour 2 tablespoons of the coconut milk into a small bowl, add the arrowroot starch, and whisk until dissolved.

2 In a small saucepan, combine the lime juice, zest, honey, salt, the remaining coconut milk, and the arrowroot slurry. Place over medium heat, bring to a simmer, and cook, stirring, until the ingredients are well incorporated, 3 to 5 minutes. Remove the mixture from the heat and allow it to cool.

3 In a blender, combine the lime juice mixture, the cashew cream, and spinach, if using, and blend until smooth. Pour the mixture into a bowl, cover, and place it in the refrigerator for a few hours to chill thoroughly.

4 Add the graham cracker crumbs to the ice cream base and freeze in an ice cream maker according to the manufacturer's instructions. You can eat the ice cream right away for a softer version, or freeze it for about 2 hours for a firmer consistency.

STRAWBERRY CHEESECAKE
ICE CREAM v

Makes 1 pint

This recipe relies on vegan cream cheese, which swirls throughout the ice cream, along with graham cracker crumbs and strawberries that have been gently simmered to intensify their natural sweetness. This pretty pink ice cream tastes like a rich slice of strawberry cheesecake. If you'd prefer to use dairy cream cheese, omit the arrowroot starch, which does not react well with dairy products.

⅔ cups full fat coconut milk (from one 13.5 ounce can), divided

1 tablespoon arrowroot starch

2 cups hulled and chopped strawberries

1 tablespoon coconut oil

¼ teaspoon salt

¼ cup maple syrup

⅓ cup vegan cream cheese, softened

1 cup Cashew Cream (page 27)

½ cup graham cracker crumbs, homemade (page 157) or store-bought

1 Pour 2 tablespoons of the coconut milk into a small bowl, add the arrowroot starch, and whisk until dissolved.

2 In a medium saucepan, combine the strawberries, coconut oil, salt, and maple syrup. Place over medium heat, bring to a simmer, and cook, stirring gently, until the strawberries begin breaking down and releasing their juices, 3 to 5 minutes. Remove the pan from heat and mix in the arrowroot slurry and the remaining coconut milk.

3 In a blender, combine the strawberry mixture, vegan cream cheese, and cashew cream and blend until smooth. Pour the mixture into a bowl, cover, and place it in the refrigerator for a few hours to chill thoroughly.

4 Add the graham cracker crumbs to the ice cream base and freeze in an ice cream maker according to the manufacturer's instructions. You can eat the ice cream right away for a softer version, or freeze it for about 2 hours for a firmer consistency.

ROASTED FIG AND CINNAMON ICE CREAM v

Makes 1 pint

Roasting figs softens the flesh and causes their sugars to lightly caramelize. Sea salt lends a nice contrast to the sweetness of the figs, while cinnamon warms the flavors of the ice cream. The roasted figs aren't added to the ice cream maker; instead, they are spread between layers of cinnamon ice cream so that when you carve a scoop, you're left with a fig-rippled ice cream.

8 fresh figs

1/3 cup plus 1 tablespoon maple syrup, divided

1/8 teaspoon large flake sea salt

1 cup full-fat coconut milk, divided (from one 13.5-ounce can)

1 tablespoon arrowroot starch

1 teaspoon ground cinnamon

1 vanilla bean

1 cup Cashew Cream (page 27)

1 Preheat the oven to 400°F. Line a baking sheet with parchment paper.

2 Wash and trim the figs and slice them lengthwise into 4 sections. In a medium bowl, mix the figs with 1 tablespoon of the maple syrup and the salt. Place the figs on the prepared baking sheet and bake for 15 minutes, or until they begin to caramelize. Remove from the oven and allow to cool.

3 Whisk 2 tablespoons of the coconut milk with the arrowroot starch in a small bowl until dissolved.

4 In a small saucepan, combine the remaining coconut milk, the arrowroot slurry, cinnamon, and remaining 1/3 cup maple syrup. Slice the vanilla bean lengthwise, scrape the seeds into the mixture, then add the bean itself. Place over medium heat, bring to a simmer, and cook, stirring, for 3 to 5 minutes until well combined. Remove from the heat and compost the vanilla bean.

5 Allow the coconut milk mixture to cool, then stir in the cashew cream. Pour into a bowl, cover, and refrigerate for a few hours to chill thoroughly.

6 Freeze in an ice cream maker according to the manufacturer's instructions. Pour half of the ice cream into a freezer-proof container. Top with the figs, then the remaining ice cream; freeze for 2 hours before serving.

MAPLE PECAN CRUNCH
ICE CREAM v

Makes 1 pint

Warm maple flavor and pecans makes for a winning flavor combination in this rich ice cream that packs a substantial crunch. This ice cream adds a nice touch to fall desserts of all varieties; try it as a topper for pumpkin pie, baked apples, or pear crisp.

¾ cup maple syrup, divided
1 teaspoon pure vanilla extract
1¼ cups pecans
¼ teaspoon salt
1 teaspoon ground cinnamon
1 cup full-fat coconut milk, divided (from one 13.5-ounce can)
1 tablespoon arrowroot starch
1 cup Cashew Cream (page 27)

1 Pour ¼ cup of the maple syrup and the vanilla into a small cast-iron skillet and cook over medium-low heat until the syrup begins to thin. Add the pecans, salt, and cinnamon and stir until the pecans are well coated with the maple syrup glaze. Remove the pan from heat and transfer the pecans to a nonstick baking sheet; place it in the refrigerator to chill.

2 Pour 2 tablespoons of the coconut milk into a small bowl, add the arrowroot starch, and whisk until dissolved.

3 In a medium bowl, stir together the remaining coconut milk, the arrowroot slurry, the cashew cream, and the remaining ½ cup maple syrup. Place the bowl in the refrigerator, cover, and chill for a few hours.

4 Freeze the mixture in an ice cream maker according to the manufacturer's instructions, adding the pecans during the final 5 minutes of churning, breaking them apart with your hands into smaller pieces as they go into the machine. You can eat the ice cream right away for a softer version, or freeze it for about 2 hours for a firmer consistency.

CHOCOLATE CINNAMON TOASTED COCONUT ICE CREAM

Makes 1 pint

For a simple chocolate ice cream, you can eliminate the toasted coconut and cinnamon, but I highly recommend giving this elevated chocolate recipe a whirl. The flavors work well together to create a warm, nutty profile, and the toasted coconut adds the slightest crunch and texture to the otherwise creamy ice cream.

5 ounces dark chocolate

1 teaspoon ground cinnamon

2 tablespoons honey

¼ teaspoon salt

1 vanilla bean

1 cup full-fat coconut milk, divided (from one 13.5-ounce can)

1 tablespoon arrowroot starch

1 cup Cashew Cream (page 27)

½ cup shredded unsweetened coconut, toasted (page 24)

1 In a double boiler set over low heat (or metal bowl held over a pan of simmering water), melt the chocolate, stirring constantly to avoid scorching. Once the chocolate is completely melted, add the cinnamon, honey, and salt and mix well. Slice the vanilla bean lengthwise and scrape the seeds into the chocolate mixture.

2 Meanwhile, pour 2 tablespoons of the coconut milk into a small bowl, add the arrowroot starch, and whisk until dissolved.

3 Add the remaining coconut milk and the arrowroot slurry to the chocolate and stir to incorporate. Remove the pan from the heat and allow the mixture to cool.

4 In a large bowl, combine the chocolate mixture and the cashew cream, mix until the ingredients are well incorporated, then cover and place in the refrigerator for a few hours to chill.

5 Freeze in an ice cream maker according to the manufacturer's instructions, adding the toasted coconut during the last 5 minutes of churning. You can eat the ice cream right away for a softer version, or freeze it for about 2 hours for a firmer consistency.

MINT CHOCOLATE CHIP ICE CREAM

Makes 1 pint

No frozen treat cookbook would be complete without a recipe for mint chocolate chip ice cream. Of course I turned the recipe entirely on its head, even adding spinach to color it green. This is optional, but it's so much fun to serve scoops of this ice cream and have your guests guess how it got its vibrant color.

1 cup full-fat coconut milk, divided (from one 13.5-ounce can)

1 tablespoon arrowroot starch

1 cup chopped fresh mint leaves

1 teaspoon pure vanilla extract

¼ teaspoon salt

½ cup honey

½ cup loosely packed spinach (optional, for color)

⅛ teaspoon peppermint extract

1 cup Cashew Cream (page 27)

3 ounces Maple-Sweetened Chocolate (page 19) or other dark chocolate, roughly chopped

1 Pour 2 tablespoons of the coconut milk into a small bowl, add the arrowroot starch, and whisk until dissolved.

2 In a medium saucepan, combine the mint leaves, vanilla, salt, honey, the remaining coconut milk, and the arrowroot slurry. Place over medium heat, bring to a simmer, and cook, stirring, until the ingredients are well incorporated, 3 to 5 minutes. Remove the pan from the heat and allow to cool. Pour the mixture through a fine-mesh sieve to remove the mint leaves. Compost the leaves.

3 Add the mixture to the blender along with the spinach, if using, the peppermint extract, and cashew cream and blend until smooth. Transfer the mixture to a bowl, cover, and place in the refrigerator for a few hours to chill thoroughly.

4 Freeze in an ice cream maker according to the manufacturer's instructions, adding the dark chocolate chunks during the last 5 minutes of churning. You can eat the ice cream right away for a softer version, or freeze it for about 2 hours for a firmer consistency.

VANILLA SPICE ICE CREAM WITH CARDAMOM AND SAFFRON

Makes 1 pint

My husband is Indian, and through learning about his cuisine, I've become quite the collector of spices. This ice cream, inspired by the popular Indian frozen dessert kulfi, has a soft yellow color, thanks to the saffron threads, and a subtle spiciness, though the vanilla flavor still comes across strong. When topped with toasted, salted pistachios it's a flavorful twist on traditional vanilla ice cream.

1 cup full-fat coconut milk, divided (from one 13.5-ounce can)

1 tablespoon arrowroot starch

⅓ cup honey

1 tablespoon cardamom pods, lightly ground

½ teaspoon saffron threads

¼ teaspoon salt

1 vanilla bean

1 cup Cashew Cream (page 27)

Toasted, salted pistachios for serving (optional)

1 Pour 2 tablespoons of the coconut milk into a small bowl, add the arrowroot starch, and whisk until dissolved.

2 In a small saucepan, combine the remaining coconut milk, the arrowroot slurry, the honey, cardamom, saffron, and salt. Slice the vanilla bean lengthwise, scrape the seeds into the mixture, then add the bean itself. Place over medium heat, bring to a simmer, and cook until the mixture is a rich yellow color, 5 to 7 minutes. Remove the pan from the heat and allow to cool.

3 Pour the mixture through a large-mesh sieve set over a large bowl, composting just the cardamom and vanilla bean. Allow the saffron threads and flecks of vanilla to remain. Add the cashew cream and mix well. Cover the bowl and place in the refrigerator for a few hours to chill.

4 Freeze the mixture in an ice cream maker according to the manufacturer's instructions. You can eat the ice cream right away for a softer version, or freeze it for about 2 hours for a firmer consistency. Serve with a sprinkling of pistachios.

CHAI GINGER ICE CREAM

Makes 1 pint

The combination of cardamom and cinnamon against the backdrop of chai tea creates a rich, aromatic ice cream with the spiciness of ginger woven throughout. If you like the intensity of ginger, I recommend adding a handful of chewy candied ginger bits to this ice cream. This ice cream goes beautifully with warm gingerbread or any type of fall breads or cakes (think cranberry cake, pumpkin bread, pear cake, and the like).

1 cup full-fat coconut milk, divided (from one 13.5-ounce can)

1 tablespoon arrowroot starch

4 chai tea bags

1-inch piece fresh ginger, chopped

¼ cup honey

½ teaspoon ground cinnamon

½ teaspoon cardamom pods, lightly ground

1 cup Cashew Cream (page 27)

1 Pour 2 tablespoons of the coconut milk into a small bowl, add the arrowroot starch, and whisk until dissolved.

2 In a small saucepan, combine the remaining coconut milk, the arrowroot slurry, the tea bags, ginger, honey, cinnamon, and cardamom. Place over medium heat and bring to a simmer, stirring to help the tea bags fully submerge. Cook until the mixture is a rich golden color, 7 to 10 minutes, then remove from the heat and allow to cool. Remove the tea bags, pressing out the liquid, and compost them.

3 Pour the mixture through a fine-mesh sieve set over a bowl, composting the solids. Add the cashew cream and mix well, then cover the bowl and place in the refrigerator for a few hours to chill thoroughly.

4 Freeze the mixture in an ice cream maker according to the manufacturer's instructions. You can eat the ice cream right away for a softer version, or freeze it for about 2 hours for a firmer consistency.

ICE CREAM SANDWICHES

HERE YOU'LL FIND RECIPES for four different cookie-like creations. They are meant for sandwiching ice cream, and thus I've paired them with ice creams and frozen yogurts from the previous sections. While I think the flavor combinations are perfect, please do play around: switch up the pairings, or enjoy the cookies on their own. Of course a scoop of ice cream on a piping hot, straight-out-of-the-oven cookie is always a safe bet too!

FLAXSEED WAFFLES
(with Maple Pecan Crunch Ice Cream)

Makes 6 waffles for 12 ice cream sandwiches

The first time I tried the combination of waffles and ice cream was during my freshman year of college; there was a soft serve machine in my dorm's dining hall, and my fellow classmates and I topped just about everything with a nice big twist of ice cream. I was remembering my cringe-worthy college diet when it came time to develop recipes for ice cream sandwiches, and I was overcome with the realization that this version of sandwiching ice cream between two layers of waffle might be even more ingenious than my original soft serve creation! Whipping the egg whites separately gives your waffles a soft and fluffy center, while the outside will be crisp and toasty.

1¾ cups unbleached all-purpose flour

2 tablespoons ground flaxseed

1½ tablespoons baking powder

1 teaspoon baking soda

½ teaspoon salt

3 large eggs, separated

4 tablespoons (½ stick) unsalted butter, melted

1¾ cups buttermilk

1½ teaspoons pure vanilla extract

1 batch Maple Pecan Crunch Ice Cream (page 142), or ice cream of your choice

1 Preheat a waffle iron.

2 In a large bowl, mix together the flour, flaxseed, baking powder, baking soda, and salt. In a separate bowl, whisk together the egg yolks, melted butter, buttermilk, and vanilla. Add the wet ingredients to the dry ingredients and stir until just mixed. Be careful not to overmix; the batter should appear lumpy.

3 In a clean bowl using a handheld mixer or in a stand mixer, beat the egg whites until soft peaks form. Using a spatula, slowly fold the egg whites into the batter.

continued

FLAXSEED WAFFLES
(with Maple Pecan
Crunch Ice Cream),
continued

4 Coat the waffle iron with nonstick cooking spray if needed. Pour $1/3$ cup batter into the center and cook according to your waffle iron's instructions. Continue making waffles until you're out of batter and cool completely.

5 Take the ice cream out of the freezer to soften for 10 to 15 minutes while you're preparing the waffles. Place 2 heaping scoops of ice cream onto the center of a cooled waffle, use a knife to spread the ice cream evenly across the waffle, then top it with a second waffle. Cut the waffle into four squares. Repeat with the remaining waffles and ice cream.

6 Wrap the individual sandwiches in parchment paper and place them in the freezer for 15 minutes to harden before serving.

GRAHAM CRACKERS
(with Key Lime Pie Ice Cream)

Makes 20 graham crackers for 10 ice cream sandwiches

Homemade graham crackers are a much healthier and heartier choice than store-bought graham crackers, which tend to have an ingredient list containing mostly unrecognizable additives and preservatives. Whether swirling crushed crackers through ice cream (as with the Strawberry Cheesecake Ice Cream, page 138), turning them into a crust for Ice Cream Pie (page 198), or using them to make this ice cream sandwich, these homemade graham crackers will earn a place in your pantry. Maybe they'll even find a place at your next s'mores night!

¾ cup unbleached all-purpose flour, plus more for dusting

½ cup whole wheat flour

1 tablespoon ground cinnamon

1 teaspoon salt

1 teaspoon baking powder

½ teaspoon baking soda

3 tablespoons coconut sugar

¼ cup honey

3 tablespoons coconut oil

¼ cup full-fat coconut milk (from one 13.5-ounce can)

1 batch Key Lime Pie Ice Cream (page 137), or ice cream of your choice

1 Preheat the oven to 350°F. Line a baking sheet with parchment paper.

2 In a large bowl, combine the flours, cinnamon, salt, baking powder, and baking soda. In a separate bowl, mix together the coconut sugar, honey, coconut oil, and coconut milk, then add the wet ingredients to the dry ingredients. Mix until the dough begins to form a ball (it may help to use your hands).

3 Turn the dough out onto a floured work surface and sprinkle your ball of dough with flour. Using

continued

GRAHAM CRACKERS
(with Key Lime Pie Ice
Cream), continued

a rolling pin, roll your dough into a thin and even sheet, the width of which should fit between the tines of a fork. Use a sharp knife to cut the dough into rectangles, squares, or other shapes. Place them on the prepared baking sheet, making sure to leave room between each so they are not touching.

4 Bake for 12 to 15 minutes, until nicely browned and firm, watching carefully at the end to avoid burning. Allow the cookies to cool completely on the baking sheet. As they cool they will become firmer and crunchier until they reach a cracker consistency.

5 Take the ice cream out of the freezer to soften for 10 to 15 minutes while the cookies are baking. Place one scoop of ice cream onto a cooled cookie, use a knife to spread the ice cream evenly across the cookie, then top it with a second cookie. Serve immediately, or wrap individual sandwiches securely in parchment paper and place in the freezer for a later date.

GINGERBREAD COOKIES
(with Chai Ginger Ice Cream)

Makes 14 cookies for 7 ice cream sandwiches

Chewy, moist, and warm with the flavors of cinnamon, ginger, cloves, and nutmeg, these cookies are the perfect match for the subtle spiciness of Chai Ginger Ice Cream. The secret to these cookies is incorporating almond butter into the batter to make them soft and moist.

1 cup unbleached all-purpose flour

½ teaspoon baking soda

¼ teaspoon salt

¾ teaspoon ground cinnamon

¾ teaspoon ground ginger

¼ teaspoon ground nutmeg

¼ teaspoon ground cloves

1 large egg

4 tablespoons (½ stick) unsalted butter

½ cup coconut sugar

¼ cup almond butter, homemade (page 30) or store-bought

3 tablespoons molasses

1 batch Chai Ginger Ice Cream (page 150), or any flavor

1 In a large bowl, mix together the flour, baking soda, salt, cinnamon, ginger, nutmeg, and cloves. In a separate bowl, whisk together the egg and softened butter using either an electric beater or a whisk using a brisk whisking motion. Add the coconut sugar, almond butter, and molasses, stirring until well mixed.

2 Begin adding the dry ingredients to the wet ingredients a little at a time, stirring as you go. Once the dry ingredients and wet ingredients are well mixed, your dough should form a ball that's wet in consistency, not at all dry or crumbly. If the dough is dry, add a few drops of water at a time until you can easily form the dough into a moist ball. Cover and refrigerate the dough for 1 hour.

3 Preheat the oven to 350°F. Line a baking sheet with parchment paper.

4 Using a tablespoon, scoop balls of dough onto the prepared baking sheet and bake for 8 to 10 minutes, until the cookies are dark brown and toasty and slightly firm to the touch. The cookies may feel a bit soft in the middle when you pull them out of the oven, but they will firm as they cool. Transfer to a wire rack and cool completely.

continued

GINGERBREAD
COOKIES (with Chai
Ginger Ice Cream),
continued

5 Take the ice cream out of the freezer to soften for 10 to 15 minutes while the cookies are baking. Place one scoop of Chai Ginger Ice Cream onto a cooled cookie, use a knife to spread the ice cream evenly across the cookie, then top it with a second cookie. Serve immediately, or wrap individual sandwiches securely in parchment paper and place in the freezer for a later date.

ALMOND COCONUT CHOCOLATE CHIP COOKIES
(with Vanilla Frozen Yogurt)

Makes 14 cookies for 7 ice cream sandwiches

Creamy vanilla frozen yogurt sandwiched between chocolate chip cookies is the holy grail of ice cream treats. These cookies are chewy, nutty, and gluten-free, using ground toasted almonds in place of flour. I make my own almond meal, though you can use store-bought. The difference between almond meal and almond flour is slight; almonds used in almond flour are blanched, meaning the skins are removed. I prefer to make almond meal with almonds that still have their skin, for a higher-fiber product. The resulting cookies are airy and almost macaroon-like. To be sure your cookies are completely gluten-free, check the label of your rolled oats. While rolled oats are naturally gluten-free, many are processed in facilities where gluten products are also produced.

1 cup almonds, toasted (page 24), or 1 cup almond meal

½ cup shredded coconut

¼ cup rolled oats

½ teaspoon baking powder

½ teaspoon salt

1 large egg

½ cup coconut sugar

1 teaspoon pure vanilla extract

3 tablespoons coconut oil

2 tablespoons almond butter, homemade (page 30) or store-bought

3 ounces Maple-Sweetened Chocolate (page 19), roughly chopped, or dark chocolate chips

1 batch Vanilla Bean Frozen Yogurt (page 117), or frozen yogurt of your choice

1 Place the almonds in a food processor and pulse until they resemble a mealy flour. Be careful not to overprocess, or your flour will begin to turn into nut butter. Transfer the almond meal to a bowl, then add the shredded coconut.

continued

ALMOND COCONUT
CHOCOLATE CHIP
COOKIES (with Vanilla
Frozen Yogurt), continued

2 Add the rolled oats to the food processor and pulse a few times, breaking them up but stopping before they turn into powder. Add to the bowl with the almond meal and coconut, then add the baking powder and salt and mix well.

3 In a separate bowl, whisk together the egg, coconut sugar, vanilla, coconut oil, and almond butter. Add the dry ingredients to the wet ingredients and mix well. Add the chopped chocolate. Cover and refrigerate the dough for 1 hour.

4 Preheat the oven to 350°F. Line a baking sheet with parchment paper.

5 Using a tablespoon, scoop balls of dough onto the prepared baking sheet. With the back of a spoon, flatten each cookie. Bake for 8 to 10 minutes, until the cookies are toasty in color and slightly firm to the touch. The cookies may feel a bit soft in the middle when you pull them out of the oven, but they will firm up as they cool. Cool completely on the baking sheet.

6 Take the frozen yogurt out of the freezer to soften for 10 to 15 minutes while the cookies are baking. Place one scoop of frozen yogurt onto a cooled cookie, use a knife to spread the ice cream evenly across the cookie, then top it with a second cookie. Serve immediately, or wrap individual sandwiches securely in parchment paper and place in the freezer for a later date.

SHAKES

TRADITIONAL ICE CREAM SHAKES are heavy on the cream and sugar and can sit like a rock in your stomach. These shakes, on the other hand, are light and flavorful and work just as well for breakfast as they do dessert or anything in between. With ingredients like cacao nibs and matcha, all of these recipes contain health-boosting ingredients and plenty of nutrients and fiber to produce a treat that is both sweet and filling.

The number one requested frozen treat in our house is the Banana Almond Shake with Cacao Nibs (page 176), a sweet, creamy treat that is equally filling as it is healthful. Keeping a freezer stocked with frozen bananas and ice cubes made from coconut milk is a surefire way to always be at the ready to whip up shakes.

ROASTED BLUEBERRY SHAKE v

Serves 3

Roasting blueberries amplifies their sweetness and leaves you with a rich, bubbly syrup perfect for creating a layered shake. This shake really lets the blueberries shine, which is why the rest of the ingredients list is so simple. Use in-season, farm-fresh blueberries for the sweetest shake. I love filling my glass with a hefty pour of the blueberry syrup and topping it with blended frozen coconut milk. I then use a straw to give it a swirl, and the result is a gorgeous, show-stopping treat. You can also blend the syrup completely with the coconut milk ice cubes for a beautiful purple-hued, creamy drink.

One 13.5-ounce can light coconut milk

3 cups blueberries

2 tablespoons maple syrup

⅓ cup almond milk, homemade (page 29) or store-bought

1 Shake the can of coconut milk, pour it into ice cube molds, and freeze overnight.

2 Preheat the oven to 450°F.

3 On a baking sheet, toss together the blueberries and maple syrup until the berries are well coated. Roast for 12 minutes, or until the berries are breaking down and bubbly; watch carefully, as the berries can quickly burn. Remove from the oven and allow to cool.

4 For a layered treat, divide the berries and their juices between the glasses. In a blender, blend the coconut milk ice cubes with the almond milk until it becomes frothy, then pour into the glasses atop the blueberries. Use a straw to swirl the layers together.

5 For a blended shake, add the cooled berries and their juices along with the coconut milk ice cubes and almond milk to a blender and blend until well mixed. Pour into three glasses and serve.

GRILLED PEACH SHAKE

Serves 2

Peaches lend themselves well to grilling; grilling the fruit caramelizes its sugars and renders the flesh both soft and flavorful. The resulting intensified sweetness becomes the base for this fruit-forward, creamy shake.

1 tablespoon coconut oil, melted

1 tablespoon honey

4 peaches, halved and pitted

1 cup Vanilla Bean Frozen Yogurt (page 117)

¼ cup almond milk, homemade (page 29) or store-bought

1 Heat the grill or a grill pan to medium heat.

2 In a small bowl, whisk together the coconut oil and honey.

3 On a plate, arrange the peach halves flesh side up. With a pastry brush, brush the coconut oil and honey mixture onto each peach, making sure to coat the entire peach, flesh and peel.

4 Place the peaches on the grill flesh side down for 3 to 5 minutes, or until the fruit begins to caramelize and grill marks appear. Flip the peaches and grill for another 1 to 2 minutes. Remove from the grill and allow to cool.

5 For a blended shake, combine the grilled peaches, the frozen yogurt, and almond milk in a blender and blend until well mixed. Pour into two chilled glasses and serve.

6 For a layered shake, blend the peaches by themselves and divide them into two glasses. Rinse the blender, add the frozen yogurt and almond milk to the machine, and blend until combined. Top off the glasses and serve.

MATCHA SHAKE v

Serves 2

This is a great shake to help you start your morning off on the right foot. Vibrant green in color and full of health benefits, the star ingredient is matcha, a superfood made from finely milled green tea leaves. Matcha has greater health benefits than green tea because you are ingesting the whole green tea leaf rather than just the brewed water. Matcha is packed with antioxidants and fiber and acts as a powerful detoxifier. Although matcha powder is a bit bitter on its own, when mixed with banana, pineapple, and coconut milk, the result is a sweet, creamy, health-boosting treat.

1 cup light coconut milk (from one 13.5-ounce can)

½ pineapple, peeled, cored, and chopped (or use 1 cup prepared pineapple juice)

1 banana, frozen

1 teaspoon matcha green tea powder

1 Pour the coconut milk into ice cube molds and freeze overnight.

2 Put the pineapple chunks through a juicer and measure 1 cup of pineapple juice.

3 In a blender, combine the pineapple juice, coconut milk ice cubes, banana, and matcha tea powder and blend until well mixed and frothy. Pour into two frosted glasses and serve.

CARROT CAKE SHAKE

Serves 2

I had a bumper crop of carrots from my garden the first summer that I developed this recipe. I was trying to use them up in every way possible: soups, breads, cakes, and cookies. It occurred to me that the carrots could lend an interesting sweetness to a blended, frothy drink, and with some experimenting, I found the recipe for success. The key to the flavor is the blend of spices, which mimic the spices found in carrot cake. I always love a bit of crunch, even in my shakes, so I top this one with coconut flakes, toasted pecans, and a pinch of shredded carrots.

1 cup almond milk, homemade (page 29) or store-bought

1 banana, frozen

1 carrot, finely chopped, with 1 tablespoon reserved for serving

2 tablespoons honey

½ tablespoon ground flaxseed

1 teaspoon ground cinnamon

1 teaspoon pure vanilla extract

¼ teaspoon ground nutmeg

¼ teaspoon ground ginger

½ cup ice cubes

Coconut flakes for serving

Toasted chopped pecans (page 24) for serving

1 Combine the almond milk, banana, carrot, honey, flaxseed, cinnamon, vanilla, nutmeg, ginger, and ice in a blender and blend until well mixed. Pour into two glasses and top with coconut flakes, chopped carrot, and toasted chopped pecans. Serve immediately.

BANANA ALMOND SHAKE
WITH CACAO NIBS

Serves 2

This is the most requested frozen recipe at our house. My boys love this shake for breakfast, as a snack, or for dessert. It is filling, full of nutrients and fiber, and deliciously sweet and creamy. On top of that, cacao nibs add unique health benefits to this shake. While cocoa is cooked during its making, stripping it of more than 90 percent of its nutrients, raw cacao is packed with health benefits like iron, magnesium, calcium, and beta-carotene. It certainly earns its status as a superfood!

2 bananas, frozen

½ cup almond butter, homemade (page 30) or store-bought

½ cup light coconut milk (from one 13.5-ounce can)

½ cup almond milk, homemade (page 29) or store-bought

2 tablespoons cacao nibs

2 tablespoons honey

½ teaspoon ground cinnamon

1 Combine all the ingredients in a blender and blend until smooth and creamy. Pour into two glasses and serve immediately.

SPICY FROZEN HOT CHOCOLATE ⓥ

Serves 2

I love hot chocolate that has a kick—a sprinkle of cinnamon and cayenne pepper goes a long way in warming the soul on a blustery winter's day. But during the heat of summer, turning hot chocolate into a frozen concoction is the way to go. Here the cayenne pepper lends a depth of flavor, playing off the intense sweetness of the chocolate and creaminess of the coconut milk.

5 ounces dark chocolate, roughly chopped

3 tablespoons coconut sugar

2 cups full-fat coconut milk, divided (from two 13.5-ounce cans)

2 cups ice cubes

⅛ teaspoon ground cayenne

Whipped Coconut Cream (page 197) for serving (optional)

1 tablespoon cacao nibs for serving (optional)

1 Using a double boiler (or metal bowl held over a pan of simmering water), melt the chocolate, stirring constantly to avoid scorching. Add the sugar, stirring constantly until thoroughly blended. Remove from the heat, slowly add 1 cup of the coconut milk, and stir until smooth. Allow the mixture to cool to room temperature.

2 In a blender, combine the remaining 1 cup coconut milk, the melted chocolate mixture, ice, and cayenne and blend on high speed until smooth. Pour into two glasses and top with whipped cream and a sprinkle of cacao nibs if you like. Serve immediately.

TOPPINGS, CONES, AND MORE

NOW WE COME TO THE REALLY FUN PART—cones, toppings, and an incredibly decadent ice cream pie. This section is devoted to everything you need to take your homemade ice creams and frozen yogurts to the next level. Serving homemade ice cream in a homemade waffle cone is pretty much as impressive as it gets. Same goes for topping your frozen yogurt with homemade vegan chocolate or caramel sauce. For the grand finale, you'll find my all-time favorite ice cream recipe, passed down to me from my mom, for a decadent and impressive ice cream pie.

ALMOND WAFFLE CONES

Makes 4 cones

Homemade waffle cones are the most impressive way in which to serve homemade ice cream and frozen yogurt. Toasty, nutty, and perfectly crunchy, these waffle cones are made with almond flour, which means this a gluten-free treat. It is important to blend the ingredients well to help the batter hold together. If you're someone who prefers their ice cream in a bowl, forget the cone shape and lay the waffle over a small ceramic bowl to create an edible bowl.

⅔ cup almond flour

¼ teaspoon salt

¼ teaspoon ground cinnamon

1 large egg

1 large egg white

1 tablespoon maple syrup

3 tablespoons unsalted butter, melted

½ teaspoon pure vanilla extract

1 Preheat a waffle cone maker to your desired setting. I set mine to level 4 to achieve a toasty brown and crunchy cone.

2 Place all the ingredients in a blender and blend until very smooth.

3 Pour ¼ cup batter onto the hot waffle maker and cook for 1 minute. Check the color and cook for an additional 30 to 45 seconds if necessary. Once done to your liking, remove the waffle from the maker and use the waffle cone shaper to roll it into a cone. Place it standing up in a narrow drinking glass to help it cool while holding its shape. Once the cone has cooled, fill with a heaping scoop of ice cream or frozen yogurt and enjoy.

4 Cones lose their crispness after the first day, so it is best to use them immediately; however, the batter can be made ahead and stored in the refrigerator for up to 2 days.

FRUIT SYRUP

Makes about 2 cups

This versatile syrup can be made from any number of fruits, although I particularly love peach, blueberry, cherry, and raspberry. The yield of this recipe will depend on the type of fruit you use; if you are using a fruit with lots of seeds, such as raspberries, you will end up with less syrup after you strain the mixture. When working with peaches, apricots, plums, and other stone fruit, you can leave the peel on and simply strain it out, or you can peel the fruit beforehand. This recipe is quite simple and begs for experimentation. I love combining fruits and find that blueberry-peach is a real winning combination.

2 cups fruit (chopped if necessary)

½ cup honey

⅓ cup water

3 tablespoons freshly squeezed lemon juice

1 tablespoon lemon zest (from about 1 lemon)

1 In a saucepan, combine the fruit, honey, and water. Place over medium heat, bring to a simmer, and cook, stirring constantly, until the fruit begins to break down and the mixture begins to thicken, 5 to 7 minutes. Remove the pan from the heat and pour the syrup through a fine-mesh sieve set over a bowl. Allow the syrup to cool, then add the lemon juice and zest and stir to combine.

2 Store the syrup in a lidded glass container such as a mason jar in the refrigerator for up to 2 weeks. Serve drizzled over anything from ice cream to waffles, oatmeal, or yogurt.

VEGAN SALTED
CARAMEL SAUCE v

Makes ½ cup

When I began experimenting with vegan caramel sauce, I was convinced that my chosen ingredients would never quite get thick enough to reach a caramel consistency. But after a bit of tweaking, a little adding, and some subtracting, I found the perfect recipe that yields a thick, golden, very convincing caramel sauce. Don't be fooled by the consistency while you're cooking; it thickens nicely as it cools.

3 tablespoons maple syrup
½ cup full-fat coconut milk
(from one 13.5-ounce can)
1 teaspoon pure vanilla extract
¼ teaspoon salt

1 In a small saucepan, combine all the ingredients. Place over medium heat, bring to a simmer, reduce the heat to low, and cook, whisking occasionally, until the mixture has thickened, about 10 minutes. The sauce will look pale at first, but as you begin heating and whisking it will thicken and take on a golden color. Remove from the heat and allow to cool and thicken more.

2 Store the caramel sauce in a lidded glass jar in the refrigerator for up to 2 weeks. Gently reheat the sauce in a saucepan set over low heat before serving.

VEGAN CHOCOLATE SAUCE v

Makes ½ cup

A drizzle of chocolate sauce can elevate an ordinary scoop of ice cream into a fanciful sundae. This chocolate sauce is entirely dairy-free and vegan. While the sauce will seem a bit runny at first, a brisk whisking will ensure that the ingredients are well mixed, resulting in a thicker sauce.

½ cup full-fat coconut milk (from one 13.5-ounce can)

¼ cup unsweetened cocoa powder

3 tablespoons coconut sugar

1 tablespoon maple syrup

1 In a small saucepan, combine all the ingredients. Place over medium heat, bring to a simmer, and whisk continually until the cocoa powder and coconut sugar are fully incorporated, 5 to 7 minutes. Remove from the heat and allow to thicken and cool.

2 Store the chocolate sauce in a lidded glass jar in the refrigerator for up to 2 weeks. Gently reheat the sauce in a saucepan set over low heat before serving.

BROWNIE BATTER v

Makes one 5 x 5-inch pan of batter

Who doesn't love cookie dough ice cream? As a kid, I'd dig out all the cookie dough bites, and when I was left with a puddle of melted vanilla ice cream, I'd simply toss it. Why bother once the dough was gone? This vegan brownie batter is a nod to those sugar-laden cookie dough bits I loved as a child. The batter is nutty and moist, with just a touch of saltiness to contrast the sweetness of the dates and maple syrup. It's best when roughly chopped and mixed into ice cream or frozen yogurt. You can add brownie bits into the ice cream mixer as it nears the end of its churning, or top a scoop of ice cream with a handful. It pairs particularly well with Coffee Frozen Yogurt (page 118).

1 cup walnuts

½ cup hazelnuts

1 cup Medjool dates, soaked for 15 minutes in hot water to cover, then drained and patted dry

¼ cup unsweetened cocoa powder

½ cup rolled oats

⅛ teaspoon salt

1 tablespoon coconut oil, melted

2 tablespoons maple syrup

1   In a food processor, combine the walnuts, hazelnuts, dates, cocoa powder, oats, and salt and pulse until the mixture becomes crumbly and begins to stick together. Add the coconut oil and pulse again. Scrape down the sides, add the maple syrup, and pulse until the mixture is well-mixed and spreadable. If you have to drizzle a bit more coconut oil in to bind the batter together, do so a bit at a time.

2   Line a 5 x 5-inch pan with parchment paper and press the batter into the pan, using a spatula to spread it evenly. Chill the pan in the refrigerator for 1 hour, then transfer the batter to a cutting board and roughly chop. The chopped batter can be stored in a lidded glass container in the refrigerator for up to 5 days or 1 month in the freezer. Unchopped batter can be wrapped tightly in parchment paper and stored in the refrigerator for up to 5 days.

ICE CREAM TRUFFLES

Makes 12 truffles

Ice cream truffles are the perfect treats to have on hand when you crave just a little something to satisfy your sweet tooth. Of course the trick is limiting yourself to just one or two. It can be quite hard to stop popping these sweet little creations in your mouth. Coconut oil and chocolate combine to create a coating that hardens when cold. Experiment with different flavors of frozen yogurt and ice cream for the inside; I particularly love fruit-flavored ice creams, as they pair so well with chocolate.

½ pint ice cream of your choice

6 ounces dark chocolate, roughly chopped

¼ cup coconut oil

1 Line a baking sheet with wax paper. Using a melon baller, scoop small balls of ice cream and place them on the wax paper. Place the sheet in the freezer for at least 30 minutes.

2 Meanwhile, in a double boiler (or metal bowl held over a pan of simmering water), combine the chocolate and coconut oil. Place over medium-low heat and bring the mixture to a liquid state, stirring continuously to avoid scorching the chocolate. Remove from the heat and pour the mixture into a small bowl.

3 Remove the baking sheet from the freezer. Using a toothpick, pick up an ice cream ball and submerge it in the chocolate sauce, rotating until it is well covered. Place it back on the baking sheet and remove the toothpick. Continue until all the ice cream balls are covered. Place the baking sheet back in the freezer for at least 30 minutes before serving. Once the chocolate coating is thoroughly frozen, the truffles can be eaten immediately or stored in a glass lidded freezer-safe container with the layers of truffles separated by a sheet of parchment paper.

CINNAMON ALMOND CRUNCH

Makes 3 cups

If you haven't figured it out by now, I can hardly eat ice cream without adding a crunchy topping or two. When I'm pressed for time, a handful of toasted nuts or coconut will do, but when I really want to savor the ice cream experience, I'll whip up an extra-special topping. Cinnamon Almond Crunch is salty, sweet, crunchy, and chewy thanks to the variety of seeds, nuts, and spices. It elevates a simple bowl of ice cream, and can even be eaten for breakfast the next morning sprinkled over yogurt and topped with fruit. It keeps well in a sealed glass jar, so make a large batch and enjoy it all week long.

2 cups rolled oats

⅓ cup sunflower seeds

⅓ cup pumpkin seeds

½ cup chopped pecans

1 tablespoon ground cinnamon

½ teaspoon salt

2 tablespoons maple syrup

1 tablespoon honey

1 tablespoon coconut oil, melted

1 Preheat the oven to 350°F. Line a baking sheet with parchment paper.

2 In a large bowl, combine the oats, sunflower seeds, pumpkin seeds, pecans, cinnamon, and salt. Add the maple syrup, honey, and coconut oil and mix well to incorporate.

3 Evenly distribute the mixture over the prepared baking sheet and bake for 15 minutes, or until it is turning golden, fragrant, and toasty. Allow the mixture to cool, then transfer it to a lidded glass container, where it will keep for up to 1 week.

WHIPPED COCONUT CREAM v

Makes 2 cups

Coconut cream is the secret to a dairy-free whipped cream. The result is a light-as-air, creamy, sweet whipped cream that is perfect for topping sundaes and shakes. The key to achieving the proper consistency is making sure that you have pre-chilled your can of coconut milk so that you can skim the cream right off the top.

1 cup coconut cream (from one 15-ounce can full-fat coconut milk)
1 tablespoon coconut sugar
1 teaspoon pure vanilla extract

1 Chill a can of coconut milk undisturbed overnight so that the coconut cream separates from the coconut water. Carefully open the can and use a spoon to scoop out just the coconut cream (reserve the remaining coconut water for another use).

2 In a large bowl, combine the coconut cream, coconut sugar, and vanilla and beat with an electric mixer on high speed for 3 to 5 minutes, until the cream becomes fluffy and light, with soft peaks.

ICE CREAM PIE

Makes one 10-inch round pie

My mom makes the very best ice cream pie in the world. No matter the holiday, she always has at least two kinds of ice cream pie for dessert, and they are always gone in record time. The key to her success is the crust, which is simply crushed graham crackers, coconut, and pecans mixed with butter and then baked. The fact that she serves it doused in rich hot fudge doesn't hurt either! Feel free to experiment with different ice cream flavors for the filling; you can even layer and mix ice creams. I particularly love using Chocolate Cinnamon Toasted Coconut Ice Cream (page 145) and serving it topped with Vegan Chocolate Sauce (page 189), toasted coconut, and toasted pecans. Pure decadence!

Pictured on pages 200–201

2 cups graham cracker crumbs, homemade (page 157) or store-bought

½ cup shredded unsweetened coconut

½ cup chopped pecans, toasted (see page 24)

½ teaspoon salt

½ cup (1 stick) unsalted butter, melted and cooled

2 pints ice cream

Whipped Coconut Cream (page 197) for serving

Vegan Chocolate Sauce (page 189) for serving

1 Preheat the oven to 375°F.

2 In a food processor, combine the graham cracker crumbs, coconut, pecans, and salt and pulse until the mixture reaches a crumb consistency. Stream in the melted butter and pulse just until combined. Pour the mixture into a 10-inch round springform pan and pat it down so that the bottom is an even layer and just begins to edge up the sides. Bake for 8 to 10 minutes, or until the crust becomes fragrant and toasty.

3 Allow the crust to cool completely in the spring-form pan before adding the ice cream. For easier spreading, take your ice cream out of the freezer

10 minutes before you add it. Plop the softened ice cream on top of the crust (still in its pan). Using a spatula, dipping it into a cup of hot water to help with spreading, smooth the ice cream into an even layer over the crust. Cover the pan with aluminum foil and place in the freezer for 2 to 4 hours, until the ice cream has hardened. Remove the pan from the freezer, release the springform, slice, and serve drizzled with chocolate sauce and a hefty scoop of whipped coconut cream. If not serving right away, the frozen pie can be stored in the pan, covered with plastic wrap, in the freezer for up to 3 days. Individual slices may also be stored wrapped in plastic wrap and kept in the freezer for up to 3 days.

WITH GRATITUDE

As with every aspect of my life, many hands help to lighten the load. First, I owe my deepest gratitude to my husband, Vijay. There were many nights when dinner didn't make it onto the table (but there was ice cream!) due to a long day of recipe testing and photographing, but that never stopped him from supporting me fully.

My two boys, Vijay and Vik, cheered me on every step of the way with their enthusiasm. When I hit on a winning recipe, they let me know by demanding seconds (and thirds!). I love having their energy whirling around the kitchen.

My life is made so much easier and more enjoyable thanks to Liz Murray, who loves my boys deeply and cares for them with endless energy and creativity.

I have the deepest appreciation for my team at Roost, first and foremost my incredible editor, Jenn Urban-Brown. I owe a big thank you to my agent, Linda Roghaar, for her continued belief in my ideas.

Joey Raho helped me tremendously with his recipe testing, kitchen assistance, and culinary knowledge.

I owe a heartfelt thank you to all of my blog readers who have encouraged me and stood by me on my writing journey.

Finally, a huge thanks to the farmers of Northern Michigan and Rhode Island for supplying my family with the most delicious, lovingly grown produce possible. Every recipe I made was inspired by the bounty of my two home states.

RESOURCES

Ingredients

CALIFIA FARMS califiafarms.com. Offering almond milk that is free of additives and preservatives, Califia Farms products can be found in the chilled dairy section at many natural food stores. Look for the Pure Unsweetened Almond Milk blend, which contains only almonds and filtered water. Califia Farms is a grower-owned company that uses almonds from California, picked at the peak of their flavor.

KING ORCHARDS kingorchards.com. A family-owned and operated orchard located in Northern Michigan, King Orchards specializes in Montmorency tart cherries. You can buy frozen tart cherries from their online store, available in 12- and 40-pound quantities. If you are in the area, a visit to their farm for U-pick fruit is well worth the trip.

NATIVE FOREST edwardandsons.com. There are many coconut milk brands out there, but I prefer the taste and quality of Native Forest, which is organic and comes in BPA-free cans.

TAZA CHOCOLATE tazachocolate.com. Producing stone ground, organic chocolate made in Somerville, Massachusetts, using the highest quality ingredients, Taza Chocolate maintains direct relationships with its cacao farmers to ensure fair wages, organic cacao, and ethical labor practices.

UNCLE MATT'S ORGANIC unclemattsorganic.com. A trusted organic source for boxes of farm-fresh citrus. Visit their online store to see which citrus fruits are season.

Farmers' Markets and Pick-Your-Own Farms

USDA NATIONAL FARMERS MARKET DIRECTORY http://search.ams .usda.gov/farmersmarkets/. The United States Department of Agriculture hosts this searchable database of farmers' markets. The site allows visitors to search by zip code, state, products available, and payment accepted.

LOCALHARVEST localharvest.com. Search for farmers' markets and available CSA shares by zip code.

FARMER'S MARKET ONLINE farmersmarketonline.com. Structured as an open-air market online, this site offers produce, nuts, grains, and specialty foods from real vendors. Use this site to find small farm–grown nuts, oatmeal, rice, sauces, jams, jellies, boxes of citrus, and other regionally specific ingredients and produce.

PICKYOUROWN.ORG A national listing of pick-your-own farms organized by state and region.

Kitchen Tools

These are my favorite, most-trusted brands, the ones I use with great success in my own kitchen.

BREVILLE breville.com. I highly recommend Breville's juicers. All models offer a heavy-duty motor, are relatively easy to clean, and have large produce feed chutes to cut down on chopping/prep time.

CHEF'S CHOICE chefschoice.com. Chef's Choice makes durable, affordable, and simple-to-use nonstick waffle cone makers, which come with a cone-rolling form. They have several heat settings, which will allow you to achieve your desired level of toastiness.

CUISINART cuisinart.com. A basic Cuisinart food processor is my favorite because it is simple to use, durable, and dishwasher safe. I also use the Cuisinart Pure Indulgence 2-quart ice cream maker and recommend it because it freezes desserts quickly, offers a large-capacity bowl, and is easy to use and clean. Cuisinart makes an affordable and easy-to-use waffle maker as well.

HAWAIIAN SHAVED ICE hawaiianshavedice.com. I use the S900A Electric Shaved Ice Machine, one of the least expensive products on the market, and have been very pleased with the results. It comes with two plastic containers that you fill with water and freeze. You then insert the block of ice into the machine, and a sharp steel blade shaves the ice as it rotates. It produces fluffy shaved ice, perfect for homemade snow cones.

NORPRO amazon.com or most kitchen supply stores. The Norpro Ice Pop Maker is a very simple mold made from BPA-free plastic. The Norpro is designed to make ten ice pops, and there is a lid that fits over the top that securely keeps the sticks in place.

VITAMIX vitamix.com. I heartily recommend a Vitamix blender. It is an investment but will last a lifetime and become a kitchen staple. Vitamix blenders are commercial grade with a powerful motor that has the ability to chop, cream, blend, grind, and churn. They are easy to clean and come with a five-year full warranty.

WECK JARS weckjars.com. These are timeless, high-quality glass jars. I like using their half-liter mold jars for serving shaved ice, frozen yogurt, and ice cream; they render the perfect single serving size and showcase the vibrant colors of the desserts.

ZIPZICLE zipzicle.com. These plastic flavored ice sleeves are BPA-free and have a tightly zipping top that holds in the liquid and ensures that the flavored ice stays fresh in your freezer for weeks.

INDEX

ABOUT THE AUTHOR

CHRISTINE CHITNIS is a mother, writer, photographer, and avid home cook. She lives with her husband and two young sons in Providence, Rhode Island. Her writing and photography are inspired by the farmland and coasts of her adopted home state, though her love of the natural world dates back to childhood summers spent in Northern Michigan.

Christine is the author of *Little Bites* (Roost, 2015) and *Markets of New England* (The Little Bookroom, 2011). Her writing has appeared in *Country Living*, *The Boston Globe*, and *Edible Rhody*, among many other local and national publications.

To follow along on her adventures in cooking, gardening, mothering, and crafting, visit ChristineChitnis.com.